LIBERTY TO THE CAPTIVES

LIBERTY TO THE CAPTIVES

the struggle against oppression in South Korea

GEORGE E. OGLE

JOHN KNOX PRESS
ATLANTA

Scripture quotations are from the King James Version of the Bible.

Library of Congress Cataloging in Publication Data

Ogle, George E   1929–
    Liberty to the captives.

    Includes bibliographical references.
    1. Ogle, George E 1929–   2. Missionaries—
Korea—Biography.   3. Missionaries—United
States—Biography.   4. Civil rights—Korea.
5. Christianity and democracy—Korea.   6. Korea—
Politics and government—1960–   I. Title.
BV3462.034A34   266'.009519'5   76–48578
ISBN 0–8042–1494–8

Printed in the United States of America

DEDICATION

I dedicate this book to seven courageous women. Their husbands were unjustly accused of treason, tortured into "confession," and cruelly hanged. Never were they allowed to defend themselves. The wives spoke out the truth attempting to serve not only their husbands, but justice and freedom as well. For their courage they, too, were arrested and beaten.

It was my honor to know these women and be a pastor to them. They are:

Kong Soon Hi, wife of Woo Hong Sun
Lee Chong Sook, wife of Lee Soo Pyung
Pai Soo Ja, wife of Suh Do Won
Shin Dong Sook, wife of To Ye Jong
Lee Yong Gyu, wife of Ha Chae Wan
Kim Jin Saing, wife of Song Song Jin
Yu Sueng Ok, wife of Kim Yong Won.

ACKNOWLEDGMENTS

Many people have contributed to the writing of this book. There have been hundreds and even thousands of factory workers in the Inchun, Pupyung, and Yongdongpo areas of Korea who have allowed me in some way to participate in their lives. Not only did they teach me about the human-social dimensions of Korean industrial development, they also were the means through which I came closer to Jesus Christ. Likewise, there are labor union leaders whom I want to thank. Their dedication to justice for the workers even in the face of strong political pressures and personal dangers has acquainted me with the real dynamics of the Korean labor movement.

And more than anyone else, I want to thank the brothers and sisters with whom I worked in Urban-Industrial Mission. Never have I worked with such dedicated and stimulating people as Cho Sung Hyuk, Cho Wha Soon, Yu Hong Shik, Won Yong Whon, and Choe Yong He of the Inchun Mission and Kim Kyung Nak, Cho Che Song, and Ahn Kwang Soo of Yongdongpo. For almost fifteen years of my life, I gained sustenance from their love and patience.

I am also grateful to the many missionary brothers and sisters who, along with the Korean Christians, are committed to the preaching of Christ's gospel and the establishment of his justice. During my last days in Korea, the communion with my fellow missionaries gave me strength.

There are so many more to whom I would like to say thanks: the pastors and people of the many Methodist, Presby-

8

terian, and Catholic churches whom I know have been praying for me; the clergymen and students who have suffered imprisonment and even tortures for their faith; and their very beautiful wives and mothers who stood firm in support of their loved ones.

I am grateful to my wife and four great children who have gone through the anxieties of the last couple of years with real trust and humor.

Finally, I want to thank the dean and faculty of Candler School of Theology of Emory University for welcoming us in our time of need. I especially want to express my gratitude to Doctor Theodore Runyan and Professor Don Saliers for reading and correcting the manuscript for me. And, of course, my many, many thanks to Ms. Susan Peller who did all of the typing.

CONTENTS

INTRODUCTION

During the 1960's, South Korea came to the attention of the world because of its success in economic development. The real uniqueness of Korea, however, was not its economic development but the fact that economic development was being achieved in a democratically oriented political system. The 1963 constitution had established democratic institutions and processes which provided the political environment for the economic successes. The Korean people had long worked for the day when they could create a democracy in their land. In the 1960's, it looked like they may have been on their way.

In 1972, however, this unique achievement of combining economic development and political democracy was destroyed. In October of that year President Park Chung Hee, in the absence of any internal or external emergency, declared martial law. Under the threats of guns, tanks, and armed soldiers, he abolished Korea's democratic constitution and democratic political processes. In their stead he established a military dictatorship with himself as a one-man dictator.

Since then, Korean society has been in a state of constant conflict and turmoil. The people of Korea have not passively accepted Park's unilateral destruction of democracy. Students, universities, newspapers, labor, and churches have openly protested, demanding a restoration of the 1963 democratic constitution. Park responds to this by increasing his suppression of all opposition. The chief instrument he uses to keep his people in line is the Korean Central Intelligence Agency (KCIA). The

KCIA operates much as the secret police of Russia. Nothing is out of its jurisdiction. The mass media are censored; labor is controlled; business is put under surveillance; foreign embassy people are followed; and plainclothesmen monitor Christian worship services.

Still the people have not backed off. Their cries for freedom from the Park system continue. By mid-1974 hundreds had been arrested and sentenced to long prison terms. Many of those imprisoned were Christians, for in Korea Christians have long been in the fore of the anti-colonial and pro-democratic movements. Ten colleagues of mine in Urban-Industrial Mission were among the arrested. They had been harassed and beaten by the KCIA because they had had the courage to try and protect the rights of poor people in the slums and workers in the factories. The KCIA accused them, as it does all the opponents of the Park regime, of being Communists.

I, along with many other missionaries, Protestant and Catholic alike, became involved in supporting the Korean Christians as they fought for justice and human rights. Under the circumstances that exist in Korea, we missionaries felt that it was incumbent upon us as followers of Jesus to stay in close communion with our fellow Christians. We could not disassociate ourselves from their sufferings merely because we happened to carry a foreign passport.

Like the Korean brothers and sisters, we were put under the surveillance of the KCIA and treated to some of the same harrassment, although the KCIA is always much more cruel to their own people than to foreigners. I was first arrested in October of 1974. The KCIA demanded that I sign a statement promising to obey all of the policies of the Park government. I refused. They released me after a day and night of continuous interrogation, but two months later I was again "detained." This time the authorities demanded that I write an apology for two sermons that I had preached. In the sermons I had spoken of the injustice and cruelty of the KCIA. When I again refused, I was put under house arrest and then forcefully expelled from Korea. I had been a missionary in Korea for almost twenty years.

This book is the story of my life as a missionary in Korea. The main focus is in the last three chapters which tell of my ministry in 1974, my arrest by the KCIA, and my subsequent expulsion from Korea. However, to understand how that situation arose and my involvement with the Korean Christians, it is important to understand the ministry in which I was engaged in the early years of my stay in Korea and it is also necessary to know something of the political conflict that has wracked Korea during the last three years. Therefore, in the first three chapters I have dealt with my ministry in Inchun from 1961 to 1971. That ministry is called Urban-Industrial Mission (UIM). In the next three chapters I talk about the *Yushin* system of dictatorial government that Park established in October of 1972. The final three chapters relate in detail my experiences as a missionary in 1974 that culminated in my deportation from Korea.

I hope these pages will communicate to the reader something of the Korean Christians' witness to Christ. I believe that witness is important for all Christians of today. I also hope my words will help stimulate discussion about the role of missionaries living in the poor nations of the world. I believe that today, perhaps more than ever, the Christian churches of the world need to be engaged in international mission. I hope our experiences over the last fifteen years will help encourage a greater mission effort.

LIBERTY TO THE CAPTIVES

1
FIRST BEGINNINGS

Six months after Dorothy and I were married, we were on our way to Korea. I had spent three years there as a K3 under the Methodist Mission Board and had fallen in love with the place. Dorothy knew even before we talked of marriage that I wanted to go back, so when she did say "yes" she was saying yes to both marrying me and going to Korea as a missionary.

After language study in Seoul, in the fall of 1961, we were sent to Inchun to begin a ministry of Urban-Industrial Mission. We found ourselves a small house in the center of the city. Our house, like all Korean houses, was uncluttered by furniture. We ate, slept and played on the floor. Korean floors are heated by a fireplace under the front part of the room. On cold winter nights sleeping on a warm *ondal* floor is a real treat in comfort. At first Korean food was hard on our taste buds that had been raised up on bland American meat and potatoes, but gradually we came to thoroughly enjoy Korean food with all of its hot pepper, garlic, onions, ginger, sesame and sauces.

Our four children, Martin, Kathy, Karen, and Kristine, were born in Korea, and since they were the only foreign children in the city they quickly learned Korean from the other children in the community. The first few years of their education were in the *Sae Pyul* (New Star) Primary School. At home, Dorothy supplemented their Korean studies with English lessons. Dorothy also helped out at the Inchun Christian Hospital and taught English at the school where our children attended.

My assignment was to do Urban-Industrial Mission (UIM). It was a new type of ministry for the Korean church. Since we knew very little about the work of labor and industry, we spent the first few months walking around to every factory and labor union office in the city. There were two of us, Mr. Cho Pyung Hun and I. Pyung Hun was my language teacher.

Any kind of freedom in the Korean language takes years and years of study and exposure. In 1961 I was anything but fluent. For an adult man to speak like a child was a cause of deep embarrassment not only to me, but also to those whom I visited. Yet there was no other alternative. I had to gain some clues as to what Inchun was like. I had to meet people and I had to be in the right place to receive guidance. At the very least, this approach proved to be excellent exercise and a remarkable stimulus for language learning.

At the same time as the leg work was being done, Pyung Hun and I were drawn into an already existing program. Inchun's East District superintendent, Rev. Cho Yong Ke, asked us to come to the services he held every Wednesday in the Han Kook Machine Shop. About fifteen men gathered in a small quonset hut. A hymn was sung and Rev. Cho prayed and preached. Everyone shook hands and the meeting was adjourned. Being a very busy man, Cho decided it would be good for Pyung Hun and me to take over the work. After a couple months of holding services together, he turned to other tasks and by default the two of us were launched on a program before we knew in which direction we wanted to go.

Not long after that a zealous young Christian engineer in the plant suggested that, if we really wanted to preach to the workers, we could do so at lunch time in the cafeteria. We could first eat with the men and then have a meeting at one end of the hall. This young man made all the arrangements, and on February 27, 1962, at twelve o'clock we went to the company dining hall to eat a bowl of rice soup with the workers. After eating, seven or eight of us went to one end of the hall. Rev. Cho Yong Ke returned for the occasion. He was the speaker. He preached for fifteen minutes on forgiveness and the need for faith in Christ, and then asked for questions or comments. There were none.

The next week it was my turn. I had prepared a talk, but even so my broken Korean must have been nearly unintelligible. Nevertheless, we had a gathering of about forty men. I chose to talk about "Why We Work." The response I received from the audience was the same as that received by Rev. Cho the week before: nothing. Finally one of the good Christian brothers asked what I thought about drinking and smoking— the inevitable question in Korea. What could be said about such a topic? Nowadays things have changed considerably, but in 1962 to have suggested that drinking or smoking does not necessarily constitute a sin would have been a heresy of serious proportions. I improvised. I claimed that neither smoking or drinking was of any importance. First came the question of belief in God. If one believed and his faith allowed him to smoke and drink then he was free to do so. This begged the question. The Christians were certain that if one really believed, he would give up these vices. The non-Christians were still uncertain whether they could drink or not if they went to church. The tenor and caliber of our lunch hall discussions never really exceeded this level. A few questions were directed towards a comparison of Christianity with ancestor worship and Buddhism, but these, as with most of the questions, were from the few Christians in the group. The others were passive. After two or three months of this, even the Christians found it hard to dream up questions. We were unable to get off the ground.

A long drought hit Korea in 1962. Electricity was rationed. For three consecutive Wednesdays the factory did not get electricity, so there was no work. Taking advantage of this rather dubious opportunity, we disengaged ourselves from the lunch room discussion sessions. The experience had not been exactly enjoyable. Each Wednesday we took ourselves to the plant by sheer will power. To stand in front of those men and talk and be met with strong silence or by questions my poor Korean could not understand was something I did not look forward to, yet it was the only opening we had at the time and so there was no way of avoiding it. Several benefits did accrue, however. We got to know quite a few of the men, and we became acceptable visitors to the factory. And probably most important of all, the discipline and the challenge of standing on one's feet and trying to communicate, though nerve-wracking, gave birth by degrees to a new "feel" for the men with whom I was talking. I developed a new confidence to continue to search.

The lead for our next step came from another of the Christian workers: "Most of the men do not come to the dining hall. They bring their lunches and eat right in the shop. Why not have your discussions there?" So, with the help of this young man and another worker, we got permission to visit the plant floor during lunch time. As soon as the lunch whistle blew, we went around to each little group of men as they sat eating their lunches. We told them we would like to talk with them after they had eaten. Much to our surprise sixty of about one hundred men came over to where we were waiting. A local pastor, Rev. Kim, and I were first introduced by one of the young workers who was helping us. Then we introduced ourselves in this way: "We are Christian ministers and would like to talk with you about any question or problems that you would like. We don't intend to preach, but we will try to honestly discuss anything you want to. We will come each Wednesday for six or seven times only. If you want to do it, good. If not, that is all right too. It's up to you."

The response was favorable. Did being in the familiar surroundings of the plant floor put them at ease? Or did the fact that everyone there was a buddy allow them to be less inhibited? Whatever the reason, questions and opinions came freely and discussions were quite lively: "Why are there so many different churches (denominations)? What is your stand on birth control? How do labor unions operate in America? Is there really a God? Isn't that a fiction of the church? When do you think war will break out again?"

The questions of one hour became the topic for discussion at the next hour. One of us ministers would speak for about ten minutes trying to bring out the issues and explaining our point of view. Then it was opened up for anyone to throw in what he pleased. After Rev. Kim talked about Christianity's relation to other religions, one fellow replied, "Don't religions change with the times? Once we had Buddhism and then Confuscianism and Spiritism and now Christianity." Another fellow agreed. "That's right. There is no one true religion. They only fit certain times and places." Rev. Kim said that might be true for other religions but not Christianity. "Christ," he claimed, "does not change. There are differences of expression, but basically it is the same." "Perhaps you are right," the reply came back, "but your gospel is too far beyond us." "What do you mean?" "The church always talks about heaven and how to get there, but working in a place like this I can't even think of heaven let alone work on getting there." Rev. Kim tried to explain how one could actually know Christ anywhere, but in fact his explanation was off the track and ended up with a clean dichotomy between the physical and spiritual worlds, thus confirming the worker's claim that there was little chance of his getting to heaven. Over and again this dualistic theology has been a thorn in the flesh. The spiritual-mental is real and is valuable per se. The material and physical is inferior or evil.

On another occasion we went over the works and failures of labor unions. "How much does an American worker make?" "Oh, about $500 per month." "That's over ten times more than we make. How do they get so much?" "There are a lot of reasons. One of the important ones is their strong labor unions. Do you all belong to a union?" "Yes, we all belong, but our unions don't do much. All they do is eat up the money we pay in dues."

"You mean you get no benefits at all?" I asked.

"Sure there are a lot of benefits. Our wages are negotiated. We get a bonus twice a year and a couple of other things."

"Yeah, but not because of the union."

"If the union is so bad why don't you guys raise a riot and demand something be done?"

"Oh, to hell with them!" The alienation of the men from their own unions was to become a familiar theme, but in 1963 and 1964 it was a new discovery to us.

Today the worker in this plant will have an average education of one or two years in high school. Just five years ago the average was second or third year junior high school. Nevertheless, even then the coherence and articulance of these men were quite impressive. Often one hears the cliche that Korean workers are too ignorant to participate in the union or in society. Our experience points the other way. They are probably as capable and alert as any comparable group anywhere in the world. The fiction about their low intelligence is perpetuated by management and some union leaders in order to maintain their own control of things.

One day when I was in the plant a group of young engineers asked if I would teach them English. They were all college graduates and highly motivated to learn the language. I agreed to help them out. I soon discovered that these young men were as interested in religion as they were in English. We would begin our sessions studying English, but usually we ended up talking about philosophy and religion. I did not manipulate the class to get around to religion. They seemed to have a natural bent to discuss such problems. It was an exciting experience to share the thoughts of these young men and give witness to my own faith.

Another ministry was opened up by a few of the Christian workers. They came and asked me to hold a Bible study for them during their lunch hour. At our first meeting, thirty Christians of all brands and emotions showed up. There was an immediate difference of opinion as to how to proceed. Some wanted a full-scale worship service. Others wanted to use the time for handing out tracts. A few suggested that we should discuss problems of the factory and community.

A compromise was reached. We would study Bible passages together. The first series of passages was taken from Second Corinthians. Each week I would choose a passage and ask three or four questions about it. I tried to balance the questions between issues related to personal faith and those connected with factory or community life. During the winter months we met on the plant floor around a stove made from fifty gallon kerosene drums. In the summer we sat on the ground outside in the sun. The fellowship created through this factory Bible study lasted for many years. It also alerted us in the UIM ministry to the fact that many Christian laymen were struggling over the problem of the relationship between Sunday morning religion and Monday morning factory life.

One day word came to us that there had been an explosion in the plant. Three men had been seriously injured. We had come to know all three of them at our discussion meetings at the factory. Immediately a local pastor and I went to the hospital and found that one of the men was lucky enough to have only lacerations of the arms and hands. The other two men, however, were not so fortunate. As they had been shoveling scrap metal into the furnace, unknowingly they had shoveled in a live hand grenade that had been lying around apparently since the war days, some ten or twelve years. The one man's face was practically gone. The other would always see as through a cloud. His eyes had been so damaged that he could never again see color, only make out shades of gray. There was nothing we could do except ask about the accident and express our regrets.

Before we left, we asked if it would be all right for us to pray. None of the men were Christians. Two of their wives were in the room. We prayed: "O God, our Father, these thy children are suffering pain and loss of health. Through no fault of their own they and their families are going through grievous hardship. Grant, O Lord, strength to conquer over pain. If possible restore these brethren to health. Give the doctors and nurses and their loved ones grace to minister to them during this time of pain. And Father, prevent that other comrades might be so injured. Help the company, and union and men to guard the health of all who work within the walls of the factory. We pray in Christ's name. Amen."

After praying we left. Two days later when we went out to the factory, we were overwhelmed by the reception. Apparently everyone in the shop had heard of our visit to the hospital. They were grateful. Most were not Christians, but still they were grateful that we had shown concern for their fellow workers. The union president came up and thanked us, and from that day on we found a welcome in the union that was to involve us even more deeply in the lives of the workers. In this instance and in countless other situations in this factory and others, we found that a hospital visit, a call at the home of a sick or injured person, or counseling with individual workers not only allowed us to be of service but was the means of grace whereby we could enter into the lives of these brethren. It also resulted in deep human relationships upon which future work with the union and management would come to be built. The individual must be known and appreciated. Individual lives are the core of labor-industrial mission. The UIM missioner has as one of his duties assisting the men and women of the shop. This involves visiting them at homes as well as at work, and especially showing concern for the poor among them.

Ministers at Labor

In March of 1962 two young men came to join the UIM ministry. Both had the same family name: Cho. Cho Sung Hyuk had been a chaplain in the Marine Corps and had pastored part time in a slum of Seoul. When he heard someone else had the same concerns as his, he decided to join us in Inchun.

This was no small sacrifice. In the Marines, Sung Hyuk had security and a good salary. Working in the shop with us, he had neither. It meant a 50% cut in wages. His young wife was quite apprehensive about the whole matter. Sung Hyuk finally got his discharge in September and moved to Inchun to begin work.

Cho Moon Gul was the same age as Sung Hyuk. Both were 27. Sung Hyuk however, had finished the seminary a few years ahead of Moon Gul. Moon Gul had spent several years in the army as a military policeman before his theological training. He was in the pastorate for only a year before he came to Inchun.

These men were assigned to very difficult situations. Moon Gul went to a steel mill, and Sung Hyuk to a plywood factory.

A pattern developed in their work that was to be repeated over and over again with other missioners who went into the shops. First there is the initial exuberance and enthusiasm of meeting the new challenge. Moon Gul's work was extremely dangerous. He worked in a scrap metal yard underneath a large magnetic crane. An engine pulling overloaded freight cars of metal whistled in and out of the yards demanding that the workers keep alert not only to the crane above but also to the rails behind and in front of them. Despite backbreaking, dangerous labor, Moon Gul maintained a mood of excitement and enthusiasm during the first month. Then came his first injury. A large lump of steel shifted when it was not supposed to, and Moon Gul's hand was underneath. Fortunately only his thumb suffered a large gash. During the next six months, four more injuries were sustained, one of them a crushed foot inflicted by a crane operator when he released the magnet too soon.

Within the first three to six months the missioner passes into a second stage. Injury, extreme physical fatigue, and a lack of "results" build up to cast the missioner into despair. Going out to work in the morning becomes such a burden that one will fake illness, rationalize the uselessness of the whole thing, and do almost anything to avoid it. Previously, the work attendance is unmarred; now it becomes punctuated by absences. The third stage appears swiftly on the heels of the second: either the missioner has to quit or the "friend" (his "back") through whom he got in the shop will have to give him a better deal. After all, he tells himself, he is no ordinary laborer and if he is to do any evangelism he needs time and lighter work.

Moon Gul and Sung Hyuk both went through this process, and only some deep sense of obligation or calling kept the third stage from being the last. They knew that to fall back on their clerical status at that juncture was self-defeat, but their aching bones and muscles demanded relief. It took perhaps another month or more of physical and spiritual suffering before they were over the hump and gained the fortitude to continue. Since then several others have failed to overcome the challenge of this third level, but it is only in the unrelenting experience of

sheer fatigue that the missioner can in anyway approximate
the constant lifetime of weariness that weighs down the workers in Korean industry. Sung Hyuk tells of the time he and a
friend stopped by to take a fellow worker out for a drink to
celebrate his birthday. The man was alone without his family,
and only 27 years of age, but his body was too spent from the
day's work; he did not have the strength to have a drink even
on his own birthday. Korean industry is grueling physical labor
in dirty, ill-managed shops. Fatigue is a characteristic of its
population. Unless the missioner can participate and persevere
in this fatigue, he can claim no right to fellowship.

Within the context of unbroken labor and weariness the
worker lives his life. It is a life punctuated by weddings and
funerals where one can get the relief of rest and liquor. It is a
life centered on hope, not for one's self, but for one's children.
One of the real spiritual revolutions that has developed in
Korea in the last decade has been the birth of a hope for the
future. The despair that regardless of what I do, my children
and I have no out, has changed to one that sees a slight possibility for some progress and improvement. This may be the most
significant revolution that the society has seen. One can endure
a lot if there is hope.

Many families are separated, with the father in the city
and the family in the country. Numerous, too, are the families
where husband and wife work leaving the children to fend for
themselves. In the West this breakup of the family is an old
tale. In Korea it is only now beginning. One day Moon Gul was
working with three women. They were breaking up large
stones. All of them were married. Their husbands worked in
other shops. To one of them Moon Gul commented, "Your
hands are almost like a man's, they are so rough and strong."
The woman began to cry. She had been robbed of her rightful
place as mother and wife and had been reduced to a daily
laborer, but for all that she was still a woman.

Factory life in Korea is a combination of man's in-
humanity to man and his deep and abiding comradeship. The
relations between the men depend to a large degree upon the

type of management supervision and the method of promotion
in the shop. In Sung Hyuk's factory, management was arbi-
trary and frequently harsh. Promotions were awarded by department heads according to their own unilateral decisions. As
a result, promotions were inconsistent and irregular, based
mainly on favoritism or "back" as it is called in Korea. On the
floor it was dog-eat-dog and everyone buttered up the boss.
There was little cooperation on the job and little fellowship
outside the shop.

However, in Moon Gul's plant, which was a nationalized
industry, the management was not only freer and less arbi-
trary, but there was the beginning of a rationalized system of
job categories and promotions. Of course, it was just a difference of degree, but still a difference that was significant. The
workers did not feel as though they were constantly being taken advantage of. Here comradeship was able to develop. The
workers in each gang and each section were apparently more
closely knit and spent time with each other outside of the shop.
Management did not pit them against each other in order to
survive. In the open hearth furnace section one of the men was
injured. After only a week, the company allowed him to return
to work even though his injured arm would not allow him to
actually carry out his duties. For more than a week he punched
in like the other men of his shift, changed into his work clothes
and went to his work section. He stood or at times sat for the
eight hours and then signed out like everyone else. Standing
doing nothing for eight hours is not easy. The other men urged
him to read the paper or take a nap. He refused. "How can I
enjoy myself while my buddies are sweating blood?" he asked.
His own financial straits made it necessary to go to work, but
his conscience would not allow him to take it easy in front of
his fellow workers.

Creating the type of atmosphere where men can have "és-
prit de corps" like this is perhaps one of management's biggest
challenges. It is possible even in difficult, underdeveloped
areas, but it does require acceptance on the part of management that the employees are men with rights, emotions, and

ideas similar to their own. The old Confucian "father-son" relationship is no longer an adequate base upon which to handle
human problems. In Sung Hyuk's plant the company president
held monthly meetings with all his thousand or so workers. The
president stayed at the home offices in Seoul, but each month
made a visit to the factory. Gathering his men together on the
shop grounds, he tried to encourage them as a father would his
son. He explained how, in fact, this factory was really theirs,
and he was there merely to help them. As they increased production everyone prospered. Once after a world trip, he gathered his men and praised them for being the real patriots of the
nation. Their cheap labor made it possible for his company to
export their products and thus earn exchange dollars which are
used for the country's economic development. The cheap cost
of their labor made them patriots. The president finished his
speech, got into a large, shiny car and took off for Seoul. The
man next to Sung Hyuk spit and said, "You bastard. We can't
eat patriotism." The laborer was not honored by being called
such a patriot. Nor did he accept the employer's patriotic view
of life. He was humiliated and embittered by it.

After the two Chos had worked for a few months we began
to think that they should now begin some "real" Christian
activity. At that time we still pretty much accepted a church-
centered approach to mission. For over a year Sung Hyuk and
Moon Gul busied themselves at evangelism and witness. When
they first entered the factory, the fact that they were ministers
was known only by the few men through whom we made the
arrangements. It was obvious, however, to those on the plant
floor that these two were not ordinary laborers. Everything was
wrong. Their looks, their language, their lack of physical stam-
ina all cast suspicion on their true identity. They were taken
as company spies, KCIA agents, or newspaper reporters. It took
perhaps a month before everyone knew their true identity, but
even then there was the further suspicion of "why?" That was
the same question we were asking. Moon Gul, Sung Hyuk, and
I felt it absolutely necessary to be inside the shop, but we were
still vague and uncertain as to why. As a result, much of our

time was consumed in carrying on activities.

One day, after a month or so of working in the shop, a man drew Sung Hyuk aside and asked him point blank if he was not a church minister. Sung Hyuk admitted that he was. "Good, we're glad you are here working with us. I'm a Christian and so are a lot of other guys around here. Let's begin a Bible class during lunch hour." Sung Hyuk hesitated, since such a move would be the same as publicizing himself as a preacher, and he was not sure what that would lead to. Nevertheless, he agreed and a Bible discussion group was organized. It lasted for only a couple of months. The few who were interested were the very conservative and zealous brethren. It took only a few meetings to open up arguments and dissentions that turned the Bible group into a fighting match.

Sung Hyuk then decided that a house-church approach would be appropriate. He and ten others covenanted to meet together in each other's homes. The time for the meetings was made to fit work shifts in the shop. Sung Hyuk and another fellow acted as coordinators making sure the times were checked with everyone. The intent was to have a freer discussion type of worship wherein the participants could openly express their fears and hopes and to center all prayer and Bible study around these specific problems. But here again the inertia of church habit prevailed. A "sermon" by Sung Hyuk or one of the other men became the central thing. The content and method easily fell into the hymn, prayer, sermon, benediction pattern. This was the "holy" way, but even so the participants honestly felt no need for an additional experience of this "holy" worship. Factory time was also unpredictable. Despite all their efforts, men frequently were unable to attend or showed up an hour or so late. The house-church concept is an effort to get worship and religious discussion into everyday family and community life of the participants, but the Korean worker lives in a one room hut jammed against his neighbor, and only a narrow path separates his house from those in front. All the noises and fights of the community are heard clearly in his own house. Everyone literally participates in everyone else's life. Neither sex nor finances nor religion is a private matter. Everything transpires in one room. Children sleep, students study, friends visit. Within this community, and inside this one room, house-church has a difficult time. Too many disruptions, too many interferences with the family, no quiet for serious considera-tion, and most of all, no release from the press of physical exhaustion that allows mind and spirit to meditate upon itself. A complete passivity or a very emotional participation is more fitting to the physical-spiritual state of the worker. A reasoned, deliberate "worship" is without experiential base. The house-church never really was a house-church, and soon withered away.

In a similar vein, during these first months and years, our attention centered around traditional Christian services and witnessing by individuals. Moon Gul circulated among the workers a variety of books about Christianity and the church. Sung Hyuk and another Christian in the shop staged debates at lunch time. On some issue of faith they would take predeter-mined positions and argue about them so that others would listen and join in. Both men used every chance to counsel and witness with non-churchmen, trying to persuade them to ac-cept Christ and identify with the church. It was not only the lack of results and fatigue that slowly but surely disillusioned us. All our methods and techniques could not obscure the terri-ble breach between the religion "we" were peddling and the "religion" "they" lived by. Ours was a narrow religion of get-ting them to accept their sin and copying us by keeping certain church rules. Theirs was the more basic and profound religion of existence, despair, and transitory hope. We did not realize it then, but theirs was more the religion of Christ, whereas ours was that of the Pharisees. The beginnings of our conversion took place through two channels, one negative and one positive.

The negative channel leading us to basic religion was the church. Christians inside the shop can be called the church in dispersion, or the people of God, or the Christian presence, or what have you, but in point of fact many of the church people in industry are none of these. They exercise a narrow, meaningless legalism or emotionalism. In Moon Gul's department there were three foremen. Only one of these actually dug in and worked. He worked even harder than his men. With humorless dedication he issued a stream of orders keeping his men constantly on the go. When work piled up, he and his men came in early and worked late, without additional pay. This foreman was a Presbyterian. His one aim in life was to be an exemplary foreman, to out-work and out-serve everyone else. To accomplish this calling he had to demand equal devotion and sacrifice from his men. They, of course, hated him with a passion. The foreman's Christian philosophy was not an individual's idiosyncrasy. It is a theology taught widely by the churches. The result, of course, is that Christians tend to be isolated and frustrated. Rather than strengthening the layman for mission in the shop, the churches often demoralize them.

Christian workers have lived in this awkward conflict for a long time. We were just becoming introduced to it, but no less than they we, too, were frustrated. The church seemed to be producing Pharisees. If Jesus had been so self-righteous about his witness and service, what fisherman or farmer or factory worker would have paid any attention to him?

On the positive side, however, at the same time that we were becoming aware of the Christian workers' predicament, a new experience drew us into the deeper waters of factory life. Sung Hyuk had been working under two false premises: one was that of being a "preacher" among workers, instead of a worker among workers. The other one was the false sense of authority that wove around him because he was an ex-officer of the Marine Corps. The workers figured he must be something special. The authority figure, however, did not last long. Within a few months it became obvious that he had no special channel to the boss, so he was on his own. At first he felt helpless and useless, but it turned out to be a blessing. One day as he was helping unload a truck of plywood, he got into a fight with the truckman. The latter was on the top of the load lifting the wood down to the men below. Instead of taking his time and doing it carefully, he threw the wood down as fast as he could and cursed the guys when they missed. Out of pure anger Sung Hyuk yelled at him, "Throw those things down right or I'll come up and knock your teeth out!" The truckman cursed him, but did as Sung Hyuk said. Through that rather mundane experience, new worlds were opened. It began to dawn on Sung Hyuk that his comrades' lives were entirely spent being oppressed by and fighting with guys like the truckman. Their "religion" and salvation had to be within the context of that life. The raw material of basic religion was not a church service, but a fight with a truckman, the web of rules under which workers' lives are ordered and the decisions made by the employer that control their incomes and social status.

Sung Hyuk's experience can be likened to a conversion experience. His eyes were opened to see the contextual situation within which the theological concept of the incarnation came alive with meaning, not in an isolated corner called religion but in the center and vortex of life is that term and its Christ to be understood. Because Sung Hyuk ran out of talk and "authority," he began to listen and participate in the shop life. For the first time he came to sense the futility that the men lived with as the foremen and management arbitrarily ruled their lives. The labor union leader had been paid off by the company, so no respite could be expected from that quarter. Where was Christ in this? What was his message? His actions? Inquiry into a new dimension of experience and theology was being born for us. Moon Gul had come to deep disillusionment with church and church ways. His course led him to disengagement from UIM, whereas Sung Hyuk's led to a new theology and a new form of involvement.

2

CONVERSION EXPERIENCE

Baptism for the Clergy

An initial experience of labor in a factory became a set requirement for missioners of the Inchun UIM. Cho Sung Hyuk and Cho Moon Gul went into the factories to help overcome our great ignorance of the labor situation. Through their experience we began to understand that it was a necessity for all missioners to have that experience. Labor in the shop has become the lifeline of industrial mission.

Through the experience of factory labor, the missioner is provided with the opportunity of being converted, away from preoccupation with himself and towards the lives of others. An ordained man or woman, to an unhealthy degree, is often wrapped up in himself. He sees himself as the bearer of Christ, indeed, as the sign of the incarnation. "Even as Christ came into the world of sinners, so I go into the world of industry" is the initial attitude. So once he gets in there, he, being "Christ" as it were, must be the guide and the light to others. He has to work harder than anyone. He must have answers. He must speak the truth to the poor benighted working class. One young man of this particular persuasion worked two months before he sprained his back trying to outwork his comrades. In such a brief time the self-appointed "incarnate one" was washed up. With each of the new staff the experience has been the same. The first three or four months are spent in physical fatigue and spiritual anguish as to "how can I be an example to these guys?" "How can I witness or lead these men to Christ?" After this initial phase one of three things happens: they quit work, they quit thinking, or they become converted. The latter is, of course, the whole intent of the work experience. The conversion is basically this: We are not the incarnate one, but rather He is to be found in and among the workers and management of industry. "We are not the channels of Grace, but rather those who receive Grace." The missioner in the first place is not the preacher of the gospel, but the one to whom the gospel is preached by his comrades in the shop. In other words, Christ is located not in me but in the common day laborer and his work place. This is a radical conversion for it gives God, His church, and salvation an identity quite different from that which has always been familiar to the new missioner. If this conversion experience does not take place, it is questionable whether the new staff member can be of any value to labor-industrial mission.

The second purpose behind hard physical labor is involvement in the personal, human relations of industrial men. The church-society tends to be genteel with strong influence coming from the women. A pastor in a week's time may spend no more than three or four hours in the company of men. All his other hours will be spent in the company of women. It is partly because of the mentality that the church and preacher are holy and thus are never to be involved in the world's passions, and party due to the feminine influence, but Christians and their clergymen have adapted a posture of detachment in regard to the world's problems. Conflict situations are to be avoided or smoothed over as easily as possible. The result is a clergy and laity divorced and hidden away from the real life of the people. The lives of the Christians and the non-Christians are formed and determined by forces that are deprived of Christian influence, mainly because the Christians feel that they have to stay clear of such entanglements. Men who would be missioners in a modern urban-industrial society need just the opposite qualifications. They need to feel at home in tense, conflict situations, for it seems that only within tension and struggle can justice and human dignity be created. Thus, a missioner is required to work at hard labor. Within the context of the primary group relationships between workers, workers and employers, workers and the community, and workers and the government the missioner begins to get a clue as to what is going on in his society. Concurrently, he comes to understand the channels within which he must operate and through which he must receive the leadings of Christ. It is true that urban-industrial society is an organized structured society, but persons live within and manipulate these structures. One must know the organization, and also be keenly aware of the crucial importance of personal dimensions and human relationships. The missioner is in the shop to discover, and, to the maximum degree possible, become involved in human relations with the workers at work and play, in the shop and in their homes. Often these are tense human relations where conflict is sharp. The missioner through direct experience has the opportunity of learning how to handle himself and how to function in the midst of strain and struggle.

The third purpose behind the missioner's required labor is so that he can get a picture of labor-management relations from the worker's side. In a rapidly developing economy, labor-management relations are important not only because of the economic implications, but also because of the social dimensions that are involved. Labor-management relations reflect a wider social context of class relationships, the relationship of the have and have-nots, the rich and poor, the elite and the common man. Furthermore, this vital relationship between the worker and his employer is almost always seen from the viewpoint of business or government policy, but seldom is it considered from the side of the workers themselves. The intent of our mission is to understand the workers' posture and to cooperate with them in increasing their influence in this relationship. Direct, continuing labor is the most accurate and perhaps the only way through which this can be done.

One year at factory labor is probably too brief a period of time. For men oriented around the institutional church and "genteel" life, as most clergy are, the total conversion of outlook that is required can hardly be accomplished in one year. Even after a year, the missioner may still be basically church-oriented both in thought and in program. Actually, the serious-ness of the situation requires a radical priest-worker move-ment, but neither our society nor our church are producing radicals.

A brief account of the laboring experience of three mission-ers follows. Most of our subsequent involvement originated from just such experiences. Dimensions of the worker's individ-ual life, the productive process, labor unions, and social justice are all illustrated in these reports. It was the depth of involve-ment of the UIM missioners in the lives of the workers that eventually, in the 1970's, brought them under the suspicion of the Korean CIA.

Woman Pastor in a Textile Mill
REV. CHO WHA SOON

About a third of Korea's industrial workers are young girls between the ages of sixteen and twenty-five. They are employed in making medicines, plastics, rubber goods, transistors, and food stuffs, but the biggest percentage work in Korea's largest industry, textiles. Rev. Cho Wha Soon is a young woman minis-ter of the Methodist Church. After serving small island churches for three years, she joined the Mission to Labor and Industry as a minister for the girls employed in the textile mills of Inchun. This report was written in January of 1967 while she was still working in the shop.

I came into Industrial Mission work without any prior preparation, so I make no claim to being an expert. I knew I would be learning as I went, but my first experience was not one to build up my confidence. The Rev. Cho Sung Hyuk had negotiated with the company about my employment, so on the day set by the company, I went to the employment office at eight in the morning. I told the young receptionist what I had come for and who I wanted to see. She disappeared for a while into one of the offices, and came back with the message that I was to wait. There were a few rough benches there, so I sat down. For two hours I sat there, getting madder with every minute that passed. That was just the beginning. When the man in charge did come out, he looked at me as though I had done something wrong, and speaking in a manner that one uses when speaking to a child or a bar maid, he told me to report over to the kitchen staff and help get lunch ready. He did not even tell me where the kitchen was. I was ready to quit right then and there. But I found my way to the kitchen. As I walked in, I was treated to some more of the same thing. A small girl, younger than I by five or six years, let loose a barrage of words as soon as she saw me. Get those clothes off and into the uniform. Get some water and soap and scrub the tables and floors. All of this was in low talk, delivered in tones that identified me as the enemy. I am not sure how it happened that I kept my mouth shut. Probably I was just too overwhelmed by it all to make any kind of a response. All my adult life I had been treated with respect. People spoke "high talk" to me. As a church pastor, wherever I went I was given the seat of honor and treated with politeness. Now within a few hours I was toppled from my high perch and made to scrub floors while a young kid glowered over me. A fire was burning inside me, but now looking back on it I know that it was an experience that taught me quickly what the life of a textile girl is like. From beginning to end she is submerged in a system that shows no respect. It is a command in sharp terms and obedience in meek subservience. My plant manages to employ almost three thousand girls. They produce a variety of yarns, threads and cotton cloth. Raw materials are imported from the United States and Egypt and some things are exported, but most of our products are sold in Korea. We are always exhorted to work harder and build up production, but the conditions in the plant do not encourage the workers to cooperate.

My kitchen duty lasted only for about three weeks. It took perhaps two of those weeks before I began to get a little confidence and feel my way around. As I did, of course, I realized that there was nothing personal in the way I had been treated.

All new people get the same treatment. Even the girl who yelled the orders to me had no official authority. After me, she was the newest one there. The staff in the kitchen is mostly middle-aged women. There are three shifts, seventeen to a shift. The ladies are all widows of men lost in the war, so their lives for the last eighteen or nineteen years have been spent in trying to keep life and family together. The only topics of conversation are money, children, and grandchildren. Friendships are strong, but the jealousies and bitterness are also deep, so that the atmosphere in the kitchen is always full of tension and back-biting. Two of the women are Christians, and a few others send their children to Sunday school, but religion is seldom a topic of conversation.

According to the agreement made with the company, I was rotated to a new section about once a month. After the kitchen, I was sent to the shipping department where the outbound goods were wrapped. Seventy girls in two shifts made the final inspections, wrapped the goods, and readied them for shipping. This is considered to be the most desirable department in the mill. As a result, the girls with the better education, senior and junior high school graduates, are concentrated here. Outside the shop these girls are the epitome of fashion. Inside the shop they talk ceaselessly of clothes, cosmetics, and men. Probably half of them are from Inchun and live at home. The other half from the country have to rent small rooms where they do their own cooking. Comparatively, there are more Christians in this section than in any other. Some of them are very devoted and evangelistic in their faith.

The next department was a different story. Here the girls work twelve hour shifts in front of machines that pull the cotton fibers into thread. The work is arduous and the girls are always in a state of fatigue. Of sixty girls in our section only eleven had above primary education. Interestingly enough, there are quite a few Christians here. Nine are Catholic and seven are Protestant. It seems that the Christian girls manage to get together in some sections.

In the winding room where I went in January, ninety girls

worked on each of three shifts. Threads used in weaving and making undershirts are produced. The noise is deafening. The lint and thread in the air turn the girls into walking snowmen in a matter of a couple of hours. There is no rest. The machines demand unremitting attention. No words are passed between the workers. The machines allow no time for talk and the noise makes it impossible anyway. Even outside the mill these girls do not seem to make the same warm friendships as the girls in other departments. Perhaps the forced isolation in the mill creates that type of individual even outside the shop, or it may be that the extreme fatigue allows no spirit for anything but sleep. When I first went to this department, my legs swelled so that I could hardly walk. My whole body ached with pain all the time I was there.

The other departments were almost as demanding. Every minute must be given to the machines. One false move can set production back by minutes or hours. One small flaw not discovered immediately can spoil the whole piece. The tension is never off. Even though I worked in the factory for only a short period of six months, I think I came to know some of their problems. The majority of girls are a little over eighteen years of age. They work eight to twelve hours a day in front of loud, noisy machines, breathing in the cotton lint that fills the air. By any measure, theirs is hard labor. Even if it is winter outside, inside, where the machines are, it is so hot the workers' sweat flows off them like rain. In this hot air work does not stop. There is not a minute's rest. Outside the shop most of the girls do not even have a family to help them overcome their physical and spiritual fatigue. They go home to one dingy, airless little room which is often used alternately by girls of other shifts. Their salaries, which average about twenty dollars a month, do not allow for an adequate human existence. Their treatment in the mill is on the same scale. Their greatest pleasure is being able to lie down and sleep.

Their monotonous life has become a habit to them, but still they have a sharp dislike for it and a sense of being unjustly oppressed by forces they can not understand. One of the results is that frequently the girls will form relationships with men they hardly know. They will spend their time and money and bodies for these men, only to be deserted in a few months. Over and over again it happens. They never seem to learn from another's tragedy. A few days ago a girl I came to know in the winding department committed suicide. She had worked and saved for four years to get her boyfriend through college. He was a boy she had met not long after she had come to Inchun. Her home was in the country in one of the southern provinces. She kept the boy, lived with him. After graduation, he threw her over for a higher class, better educated woman. She took poison and went to his house where she lay down in front of the gate and died. Tragedies like this are almost common.

In all of this what are the directions and involvements that should guide a mission that bears the name of Christ? As of yet, I am still in training, but I have come to the following tentative conclusions:

1. I think it is really necessary for the missioner to live and labor along with the girls for at least a couple of years. If the missioner is a minister, he or she should not disclose it. Once my identity became known, my relations with the girls seemed to become unnatural. This is a hindrance to my learning and my involvement.

2. The girls' lives are so monotonous, and their concept of themselves and their work so low, that we must somehow find a way to give them meaning and a sense of pride in themselves.

3. Above all, the girls want to be recognized as human beings who have some rights of their own. They want to be treated as human beings, not as work horses. Their needs are not only material but also spiritual, in that they want understanding and kindness instead of the harsh and debasing treatment that they usually get. To help this need for human relationships, we should first try to get the Christian girls there to understand the problems and to be a center around which a new bond of fellowship and mutual respect can be built. We should also develop group work for the girls, giving them an opportunity to discuss their mutual problems, take the lead in

some activity, and at least momentarily overcome the monotony of their lives.

4. Even though most of the girls have no apparent interest in the church, there are some who sense a great loss because they can not attend church like they used to. There are also others who have the beginnings of an interest, but because of their time schedules at the shop they have no way of exploring it. It would be possible for us to hold meetings that coordinate with the factory's schedule. The Christians and others who are interested could attend. The content and method could be worked out, but the important point is that they should center on questions of faith and life.

Preacher in the Maintenance Crew
REV. AHN KWANG SOO

The Rev. Ahn Kwang Soo finished his seminary work in 1964. After four years in the pastorate, he entered a large factory in the Yongdong-po area of Seoul in April of 1969. Mr. Ahn worked as an unskilled laborer in the maintenance crew until he was laid off. Though he was on the job for only five months, it proved to be a very instructive experience.

The factory that employed me was begun about ten years ago, but because of political complications following the downfall of the Syngman Rhee regime the construction remained incomplete until just last year. I was hired as one of the workers for the construction crews that were putting the building into operating order. In our crew there were fifty men. We handled almost every conceivable type of work. I carried large construction stones on my back, helped build a gate house, mixed cement, operated a centrifugal pump and filter system, and helped install the new machines in the sugar refinery. My experience is indictive of the way management was going about the job. Men with absolutely no background or experience were put on jobs for short times and then transferred without apparent reason. One of our gang was put in charge of a compression pump. He had never seen such a machine before and, therefore, he had no idea of how it operated. In the whole section there was not a man skilled at that job. One day an explosion occurred destroying the pump. The worker, of course, was held responsible and fired on the spot.

One cannot know for sure, but from the point of view of the man on the floor, it seems that management looks upon the laborer only as a number. To do a certain job, a certain number of workers are needed. The skills and use of the men apparently do not have high priority. Altogether there were eight hundred of us working, but there was no medical service at all for the injured, no bath house, and not even any decent drinking water. A well which smelled of sulphur was the only water supply for the workers, though trucks brought fresh water for the office staff.

The pay system too seemed just as haphazard. The base pay was thirty-two won per hour (about $.10), but the foreman had means of increasing it for anyone he wanted to. Some were getting fifty won per hour doing exactly the same work. It depended on whether you were in the good graces of the foreman. Needless to say, this is a source of constant friction and hard feelings.

I am no personnel man, but the importance of handling workers right and creating a good atmosphere was impressed on me one night when we were working the midnight shift. Eight of us were working in the starch sections. It involved a lot of heavy lifting and carrying. We were all ready to drop. It was dark outside, of course, and the only sound was the passing trains. This seemed to add to our depression and fatigue. But somehow in the midst of this situation a change came over us. As we were moving the heavy starch tanks, we began to joke and horse around. Our depression passed over into real enjoyment. The same work was transformed from a burden into a game. Someone from another gang happened to be nearby and wanted to know who we were trying to butter up. No one was going to put a star on our foreheads. His words did not dampen our spirits. Since we had to be there doing that work we might as well enjoy ourselves. The night's work was done in about half the time, with fewer losses and certainly with a better spirit than at any other time. When the boss came around and saw what we had done, he told us to get a couple of hours of sleep, an order which we gratefully obeyed.

I have seen just the opposite atmosphere created also. This is the more common experience, and it is usually because the supervisors make poor use of their men, and then chew them out mercilessly when something goes wrong.

Most of the men I worked with were between the ages of thirty and thirty-three. Only five of the fifty were unmarried. Educationally, seven men had graduated from high school, fifteen from junior high and seventeen had only a grade school education. One man had finished college and one man had never been to school. These men lived on the incomes they got from temporary jobs that they were able to land. The job they were holding as construction workers was also temporary. It paid them about thirty-one dollars a month, which, of course, is sufficient for only a marginal living for a family of four or five. Fortunately, some of them have their incomes supplemented by rice from family lands in the country, or by money that their wives earn through small-scale buying and selling. Nine of the men have been able to buy their own homes, small as they are. All the others, however, rent rooms in the Yong-dong-po area, but they will move from place to place wherever a job opens up. Having worked with these men and visited in their homes I know that many have a deep love and devotion in their families.

One evening as I walked home with a buddy, his wife came down the road to meet him. She carried a small baby, their first child, on her back. I could feel the love they had for each other. In other places, however, the women have to be away all day working. The children, once they get to be four or five, fend for themselves or are taken care of by neighbors. Several such women worked in our shop and did the cleaning, but they also picked up leftover scrap metal. Sometimes they picked up other things that could not be classified as scrap. Looked at from one point of view, their activities were understandable. On their small salaries no one could live, yet it was against the company rules, and it was stealing. Once I gave some of them some of the leftover wood and metal that I had been working with. A few days later, one of them came and asked if I could get her some copper tubing. I asked her how much she made in a day, and she said she made enough for bus fare plus a little bit of bread each day. "How are you going to get any copper pipe out of the shop?" I asked. She would carry it out under her skirt. (Korean style skirts reach to the ground.) The guards were not allowed to search a woman too carefully. "Where do you sell it?" "Oh, there are places." She would say no more. I told her I would give her what I could, but the material that was still good or usable I could not let her have. She left without a word. I frequently saw her gathering her "scrap." One evening as I was going home after work, I looked in the door of a wine house where the men frequently hang out. This woman, who gathered up scrap, was sitting there by herself. She had a glass of wine and was singing to herself. She was alone, and terribly sad. Perhaps the wine and song gave her wearied mind and body some relief. She was doing the best she could with the life she had.

Another problem that plagues so many of the men is the fact that they have just come to the city and have not had time to adjust to city and factory life. One of the men in our crew had been in the city for only two years. His family was still in the country. He had not been able to save enough money to rent a room for both him and his wife. Now, two years later, he finally had come to the place where he could get a room, but the glitter of the city and the charm of city women had convinced him that his rural background and his "countrified" wife would only be millstones around his neck. He decided to divorce himself from both. One day he asked me how to go about getting a divorce. By asking a question or two I learned about his intentions. I told him that I was a fortune teller and that I could read people's faces to see if they are well matched by the fates for married life or not. (Actually I had played around a little in the fortune telling business just as a hobby.) If I could see him and his wife together I would be able to tell whether or not they should be divorced. Even now many people have strong faith in fortune tellers. I also told him that if he divorced his wife he might have to pay alimony to her. In the end he rented a small room with a kitchen and brought his wife to see what I thought. After I had talked with them both for a while, I assured the husband that he and his wife were well matched and that he should not consider divorce. This plus the worry over alimony must have persuaded him. They are still living together and the wife is beginning to take on the habits and dress of the young city girls.

Economics Graduate in an Electric Shop
You Hung Shik

Yu Hong Shik is a layman who did his university studies in economics. After finishing his military service, he came to work with the Mission to Labor and Industry in 1967. He did his year's labor in an electrical equipment manufacturing company. Upon completion of his work in the factory, Hong Shik was appointed to work in programs of labor education and assistance to labor union leaders.

People speak relative to their experiences and situations. From my position in the shop as a daily laborer, I see industrial mission mainly as involvement in the labor movement in order to establish social justice. This I understand as related to the concept of the Kingdom of God. Within this society created by men, Christ's resurrected spirit struggles to complete the establishment of justice. In this way God's Kingdom is continually being built among us. It is not a place or organization, but consists of acts of justice themselves. To work to fulfill justice is then to be equated with working to establish God's Kingdom. If this be true, then what can we do in industry to participate in the creation of justice?

Two things, I think, need special attention. We can help seek out the bottlenecks and contradictions within the line of command and organization of management. And we can exam-

ine the role and function of labor unions. What are they doing?
How can we be of service and cooperate with them?

In our company the organization of management seems to
be in accordance with what the experts suggest. The line and
staff setup is exact, and its personnel is well trained. Most of
the men in middle management positions are now graduates of
technical universities, but, as is often the case, the theory and
facts operate according to separate laws. Regardless of how
well educated the managers are, or how well organized the
company is, the chain of command remains ineffective unless
there is a unity and cooperation with the men on the floor. If
one looks at our shop there are in fact two systems of command,
one that operates on top levels and another that operates below. The gap between these two results in a large negative
influence on the production and development of the whole
plant. Let me cite examples from my own experience.

In making a motor, the casing is first made in the casting
shop. Then it is sent to the machine shop for exact cutting and
polishing. I helped produce the motor case in the casting section. After the motor case was turned out, our job was to
smooth and cut out as many of the rough places as possible
before sending it on over to the machine shop. Using grinders
we cut off a lot of the unnecessary adherents, but the process
took a considerable amount of time for each piece. The time the
supervisors allowed was not nearly enough time to do the job.
Orders were piling up. The foreman cursed us and the top
officemen threatened us, but production could not be stepped
up. It happened by chance that the foreman sent me on an
errand to the drafting room. One of the men there asked me
why the work was not being turned out. Rather irritated by all
the "hell" we had been getting, I answered, "Have you ever
tried to grind the rough edges off a steel casing? It takes time!
We're working our heads off and all you guys do is chew us out."
The fellow's surprising reply was, "Well I'll be damned! What
are you grinding off edges for? The machine shop can do that
in a few seconds."

For months upon months, and perhaps even years, before

I entered the factory, the whole production of motor cases had been bottled up by an unnecessary process. Yet the official line of command never reached down to the shop floor to discover the problem. By accident we had stumbled upon the description of how the job was to be done. Afterwards we could meet our quota. The relations with the guys upstairs improved immensely. Our foreman became human and the whole section took a deep breath and relaxed. The work lost a lot of its repulsiveness. No one had actually done anything wrong. There was a difference of opinion as to how the work should be done, and no direct line of command existed that could see that the right procedure was followed. The repercussions of such a situation are immense. The constant tension and bad feelings between office people and production workers have their source here. There is frustration in both sides which closes the channels of mutual understanding. The negative effect of this on production and development of the industry is obvious. Instead of a unified organization where all participate, there are two separate ones which are often in conflict.

Let us take another example. I worked longest in the section that makes the electric core for the motors. From the machine shop come the rotors for the motor, and the lathes turned out the bar that is used. Our job was to assemble the various parts, but regardless of how we would work, the rotors and bars just could not be made to match. The bar was to go through the rotor, but it would not fit. Department heads descended upon us to investigate. A lot of heat was generated. The skill and attitudes of the workers were called into question. Threats were made. Actually, the problem was rather simple. The specifications were so minute and exact that the machines could not do the work. The operators were getting as close as they could, but that was not enough. Only after the order had been accepted, plans made and production well on its way, was the capacity of the machines considered. The men in the top positions had not deemed it necessary to consult the shop floor about the job or the machines. Over and over this drama is enacted. By now neither side has faith or confidence in the other. New machines are needed, but even more necessary is an organization where the contributions and skills of the production workers can be recognized and utilized.

Safety is another serious problem that creates tension and even hatred. It is the lack of safety devices and education that results in injury or death that causes the trouble. Often the old, dilapitated machines are manned by young inexperienced apprentices. Once a man builds up experience he moves to another company. Thus the machinists are usually the young men. There is little safety education. The company demands increased production and increased speed from the workers, which result in accidents. About a month ago one young man was made a machine operator. He had been in the shop for only two months. In order to keep up with the others and make himself look good in front of the foreman, he worked his machine at high speed. He not only turned out shoddy work, but after being on the machine for only a few days, he made one awkward movement of his right arm and his thumb came off in one clear cut. He is twenty-three years old. What kind of work can he get now? He has a family to support and long years to live. Another man was given no safety instruction when he came into the section. No one told him that some of the drums located near his place of work contained gas. He lighted his blow torch in the wrong place and was lucky to get away with losing only one leg.

Accident prevention is of particular concern in a factory, not only because accidents cause individuals to suffer needlessly all their lives, but also because the frequency of accidents creates an atmosphere tense with fear and suspicion that the top guys are earning their money through the sufferings of the workers. Just a little investment of effort and money could create an entirely new attitude toward work. At present the company sets up its organization and plans without consultation with the workers. Production and safety suffer.

The company's organization is unilateral, but on the other hand the unions, too, seem to be of a similar nature. There is little direct participation by the workers themselves. The union, which is to represent the workers in its negotiations and conflicts with the employer, is not really within the control of the workers at all. Men who are not really laborers, or who form a special class of laborers, run the union. To the ordinary worker there is the organization of the company and the organization of the union, but both are removed from him. I have heard that unions in developed countries are organizations that grow up among the workers and are responsive to the workers' desires. If this is so, they must have real life and vigor. Our union is not like that. It is a wooden formality. Yet it is still a terribly important organization. What are its problems and how can it be made responsive to the workers' demands?

To many people a labor dispute has a bad connotation, but in fact it can be a very constructive operation. From disputes evolve new ideas, new organization, new skills, and new human relations. Of course, disputes are also an efficient way of deciding appropriate wages, while at the same time protecting workers' rights. Underlying these constructive aspects of a dispute is the solidarity of the workers. From it comes the strength and power to enter a dispute. A few months ago wages were raised in our shop. The union and the company agreed on an overall percentage of increase, but the company was allowed to apply it as they wished. The result was that many men left the company. They had been given little or no raise in comparison to the other workers. One man who left was a union shop representative. He had spoken out strongly against certain practices of the company and union at the last general meeting of union officers. Both the company and union were angry. Of all the union representatives, he was the only one who did not receive a fair wage increase. It was obvious that he was being asked to leave. He obliged and quit. The union took no notice of his departure. This is somewhat representative. The union gives little indication that it wants to hear from its members. The result is disinterest or bitter criticism, and the union fails to develop any solid bargaining power. The company unilaterally does as it sees fit.

One day a large poster appeared on the bulletin board. The

company was announcing that the factory's wage structure was being switched to an incentive system. All the present classifications and allowances were being discontinued. The reason behind this move was to break up the hold that older men with seniority held on the better jobs. The aim was to move younger men into these jobs. The young men could outwork the older men, while the older men had acquired certain allowances that could be dispensed with under the new system. This system was put into effect without any prior notice or consultation. Yet the union said nothing. The workers were angry and outraged, but helpless. Instead of rallying the workers, the union pushed them further into apathy. Overnight the older men had been deprived of everything they had been sweating for for years.

There is great need for a union to act as a spokesman for the individual inside the shop. The union should be the spokesman and protector of the worker's dignity, but it is not. Each person is left to fend for himself. Human dignity gets little attention. It could also act as the channel through which the workers could express themselves, both to each other, and to the company. The men I work with are intelligent persons who could make contributions in a lot of areas, but there is no opportunity. No one outside the shop really cares one way or the other. The worker is isolated. Even his relations with his buddies are threatened by loss of status or job. He is alienated from the company and the union. The union becomes somewhat of an empty frame. Its representatives are chosen by the workers, but in most cases the job goes to the foreman without contest. That way there is no interference on the job and the union retains its organization, unthreatened by workers.

I have mentioned three main problem areas: First, the problem of poor management organization; second, the question of union isolation from its own members; and third, the plight of the individual workers who are caught underneath both the company and the union. These three problem areas define, I believe, the work task of labor industrial mission. Through study, labor, and involvement on all levels we need to help the company, the union, and the workers to face and solve their problems. We have no special authority to solve anything, but we may be of assistance in getting them to do it. In this way will we not be helping to build up justice and God's Kingdom in our land?

New Life for the Laity

Urban-Industrial Mission is very much a joint venture between full-time missioners and Christian laymen who work in industry. If leadership is concentrated in the hands of the missioners, the ministry is likely to be out of touch with the workers' factory and community life. The Christian layman contributes a balance and integrity to UIM. Before he can make this contribution, however, he may also have to go through an experience of conversion.

Christian workers experience all the insecurities and threats that their fellow workers do. A worker, Christian or not, receives a wage of approximately $40 a month. This allows for a marginal existence as long as no big expense such as sickness or school fees come along. But since these and other vagaries of life are inevitable, most everyone is in debt to some degree. There is no let-up of the pressure. The worker lives in a small two-room house, rammed up against that of his neighbor. His neighborhood is a forest of small huts separated only by winding paths. There are, of course, no playgrounds. In the factory he moves according to the command of the foreman and department head. His place of work is dirty, noisy and extremely dangerous. He has nothing to say about what or how he works. The union that is supposedly there to protect him apparently could not care less whether he lives or dies. But in all of this there is one aching drive: to make more money. Money means freedom. It means education, self-respect. Religion and church are important, but life now and the hope that maybe "my lot" will improve are more immediate, more demanding, and more important.

One might argue that religion should not be spoken of as though it were outside the demands of life, but in fact that is the category in which both the layman and the church operate.

The position of the church can be characterized by the saying that Christians are to be in the world but not of it. This is interpreted to mean that of necessity since we are born into this world we are physically in it, but our minds and souls all belong to the higher realms of God.

Christians' ties with "the world" are two: first, we are to witness and evangelize so that non-Christians will have a chance to escape from the world, be saved and go to heaven. In a sense this urgency toward evangelism of this nature has been the genius and strength of Korea Protestantism. Every Christian feels himself under restraint to witness.

Second is the command to be an example to others. Since we are Christians, we should be more righteous, more honest, more diligent than the non-Christians who are children of darkness. The badge of this exemplary life is abstaining from alcoholic drink, but it also motivates some Christians to work overtime for free, to work without a break, to do hard, dirty jobs that no one else will do, and sometimes it leads to an excellence in skill. But this type of attitude has begun to crumble. It is becoming obvious to everyone that something is awfully wrong. The compulsion to witness and be exemplary has mainly resulted in isolated, bewildered Christians. Many laymen are deep in a crisis of faith. The categories of "conversion out of the world" and "salvation in heaven" no longer have the power of persuasion. Though the Christian desires to retain his faith in God through Christ, increasingly he questions what the church and Christian faith are really about. Increasingly the attacks of industrial life undermine the significance of their understanding of Christianity.

One of UIM's major priorities has been training for the Christians who work in Inchun's factories. The questions around which the training has evolved are these: Without discarding one's personal experience of faith in Jesus as Saviour, how do we recognize him in our factory life? Where is Jesus in the production process? In the relationships between employer and employee, between worker and worker? These are the areas that actually control the Christian's life, and it is just not clear what Jesus has to do with any of them.

Laymen need to be converted to the position where they can see the social Jesus. Jesus, while being the son of God, was a human being, as we are, who lived in society, who experienced the threats of physical life and was killed by the authorities that ruled his society. Jesus was an individual person and a social person. His salvation, likewise, embraces both the individual and society.

Christian workers in Korea have seldom been told about the man Jesus and the efficacy of his life, death, and resurrection for the salvation of their daily factory life. The church generally teaches them about a mysterious, abstract Jesus who can take their soul to heaven. To convert one's concept of Jesus so as to accept his human and social character is not always easy. Sometimes it occasions real spiritual suffering for the believer.

Below are reports of three Christian laymen who went through a training course given by the Inchun UIM. They were members of a group of twelve men and women. Each person was a Christian who worked in one of Inchun's factories. When the course was completed, they were commissioned as "factory apostles" in a service lead by the Methodist Bishop and the Moderator of the Presbyterian Church.

Report #1 by Yun Ki Lee

The Han Kook Company has two plants in Inchun. The main shop produces plywood for export while the second plant is mainly used as a dryer and for production of plywood for domestic markets. About two thousand men and a thousand women work in the factories. Almost everyone works a twelve hour shift, with shifts changing every seven days. My own work is in the drying section of the second plant.

Along with eleven other Christian workers, I took part in the special training course that resulted in our commissioning as "factory apostles." Perhaps the biggest thing that I got out of our sessions was the sense of calling that helped me see that I had a mission in my own shop. I could not passively wait for a pastor or some other outsider to come into the shop to preach or hold meetings. This was highly unlikely in any case and probably of very little value even if it could be done. If mission is to be carried out it must be by the Christian worker who is in the same place of work sharing the same kind of life as the non-Christians. Words are important to the witness, but the words and acts have to have an obvious unity.

To put my new convictions into action, first I began to visit the homes of the men with whom I work. I had been in only one or two of their places since it is not common for us to visit back and forth. Like my own, the houses were all one- or two-room, small shacks huddled into a small area. I am not sure I learned anything new in my visits, but they did bring me closer to several of the men. I also tried to make a call on anyone in the shop who was sick or injured. If he were a Christian, I would have a word of prayer. If not, I would offer some words of comfort and if an opportune time presented itself I would use some story or passage from the Bible.

A third thing I tried was assistance to men who for some reason were off work for a period of time. All kinds of unexpected accidents can keep a man from work, and to miss work means a loss of income which in many cases means less or no food. In these cases there is not much I can do, but I tried to help a couple of fellows get their family problems settled in order that they could get back to work. The fourth thing I ventured into was discussion with the men in my gang about labor union problems and our relations as workers with the foreman and supervisors. Nothing formal, but as we ate our lunches I'd broach the subject. It is not hard to get men going on subjects like these. I learned considerably about the way others were thinking.

The response and welcome I received as I tried to give witness to Christ in these several ways was encouraging. I learned a lot about men whom I had been working with for years. Frequently I work twelve hours and more a day so I cannot make many visits, but small though it is, in this way I try to serve Christ. Many of my fellow Christians, however, do not agree with me. "What good is it for you to knock yourself out? The problem is money, not visiting and talking," or "This world is corrupt and there is nothing you can do about it." Certainly their evaluation of the situation is right. Money in the form of increased wages could solve many of our problems. What we can do about wages, I am not sure, but I see no reason why we cannot help our fellow workers who are suffering. We are not inert. Actually, several other younger men began talking about joining with me to try to serve others in our shop.

Before we were able to go far on that line, however, the focus of my attention was abruptly changed. For two months the company failed to pay us our wages. In concrete terms this meant hunger and debt for us workers. The company made no explanation except that they were having problems. The attitude shown to us on the floor when we asked the foremen or supervisors was, "If you don't like it get out. There's a lot of men who would be glad to take your place."

At the same time, it was discovered that the company was actually contracting out new work to smaller places that paid their workers even less than what we received. Everyone was fighting mad. Our wages were two months in arrears. We were told to like it or lump it, and at the very same time they were using money that should have come to us to pay other people to do work that was being taken away from us. But who was there to stand up for us? No one would say a thing to the plant manager or department heads. Then very unexpectedly the manager held a meeting and told us about subcontracting the work. After he finished talking, I did something I had never before done in my whole life. I stood up in the middle of all the men and confronted the plant manager. "If you take that attitude, there is going to be trouble. We too have to live. How can anyone live for two months without any income? By contracting out our work you make our life the more miserable. Even now we can only make ends meet if we work three or four hours of overtime every day."

When I said this my supervisor yelled at me, "What right do you have to talk like that? You don't even come to work on

Sunday. If someone who comes out to work all the time talks like that it's one thing, but a guy like you who takes off one day each week should keep his mouth shut!" A foreman joined in, "Guys like you who don't pull their share make the company contract out work!"

I yelled back, "Don't give me that crap. The company can't pay our wages because I don't work on Sunday? You contract out our work because I don't work on Sunday? Bull! I'd like to talk with the president of this company and tell him what's going on." This blew the top off things. Everyone started shouting and yelling. We almost had a riot.

Later in the day there was a big meeting of the management to consider the situation. I was called to give an account for what I had said earlier. I reiterated my stand of the morning: "To tell us that you can not pay our wages and at the same time contract out our work is foolish. And in the face of it all to ask us to be loyal and work faithfully is to treat us with contempt."

I was interrupted. "Why did you say there would be trouble if the wages weren't paid? What kind of trouble?"

"How can you treat us like this and not expect trouble? Our lives are completely tied to this factory. Our very existence depends on it. What endangers it, endangers us. Yet you seem to care nothing for the threat you pose to our lives when you give other people our work and refuse to pay us. Wouldn't it be better to be on the level with us?"

I went on then to ask a question of the plant manager. "Is the company really in trouble because some of us do not work on Sunday?"

His reply was very cold. "I never said that. It was merely an illustration. We don't need to explain to you about how we manage things. That is not your concern. As far as Sunday work is concerned, we do not say you have to come to work, but when we are busy here why can't you come out to work during the day and go to church early in the morning or late at night? If your neighbor's house caught on fire at church time, you'd put out the fire and then go to church, wouldn't you? At a time like right now when we are in tough straits, we can't rest for even an hour."

The next day I was informed that I had better write an apology for the way I had spoken to the plant manager. I refused. When my foreman heard that I would not apologize, he asked me to do it for his sake. Otherwise he would be in bad trouble for not being able to control his men. I told him that I had nothing to apologize for, but if he was in trouble because of me, I said I would write the apology. I wrote it and then went and apologized to both the plant manager and my supervisor. The former said that he had intended to discipline me, but since I had apologized, he would not do it. The facts were that there were no rules covering my offense so he did not know how to discipline me. He did, however, transfer me to another section.

I thought that the matter was closed when at long last our wages were paid and the subcontracting was discontinued. I was wrong. We have a labor union in our factory. It's not much, as it is pretty well dominated by the company, but each year we go through the motions of choosing our representatives and officers. To my surprise and the company's displeasure, I was chosen as the union representative for our section. I was the only non-foreman among all the union officers. At the same time I was still not working on Sunday. I had always tried to keep Sunday as a holy day for rest and church. I was not convinced that the absence of the few Christians worked a hardship on the company. Now I was to be really put to the test. A new policy was announced. Anyone not reporting for work on Sundays would not be given overtime work. My income of $44.44 per month consisted of about twenty-five dollars from regular wages and the remainder was income from overtime work. My family could not live unless I worked overtime. To give in and work Sundays meant I would have to bow my head to the force of the supervisors with a certain loss of prestige among the workers. To hold out was to submit my family to suffering. I decided to hold out in the hopes that something would happen. Living on half-salary is no picnic. Pressures built up in the shop. I felt I was being forced out, but I had nowhere to go. Just when I reached the end of the rope, help came. Rev. Cho Sung Hyuk who works with us in Industrial Evangelism was able to work out a compromise with the plant manager. Again I was transferred and put on the swing shift. My income was a little less than it had been, and at times I would have to work on Sundays. I was worse off than I had been, but not nearly as bad off as I could have been. I feel I still have a ministry in the factory. Perhaps the Lord can even use me in the union.

Report #2 by Kum Ja Pyun

Chosen Textile Mills are located on the outskirts of town, not far from an American Army base. At one time under the Japanese it was a large, prosperous concern, but over half of its buildings and facilities were completely devastated by the war of 1950. The remaining parts were again put into order after the war and production began. Even today the five hundred or so people who work in the plant do so in the shadow of war ruins. The company is owned by a man who has large holdings in a variety of industries, but he has not seen fit to renovate the Inchun mill. The conditions are depressing and the work hard. As in all Korean textile mills, the work is done by young girls, many of them right off the farm. They live one, two, or a dozen in a rented room, cook their own meals, and work a shift of eight to twelve hours a day. In return they receive at the end of each month a wage of about $18.00. The following is the witness of a young woman in this factory.

The commission given us as "factory apostles" was a large one, one for which I knew myself to be inadequate. I was afraid. I prayed that God would use me. I knew I had to do something. The first thing that came into mind was visitation of the sick and calling on the families of the girls who lived in the neighborhood. After a visit, I tried to locate the whereabouts of the girl in the mill and talk with her whenever I had a chance. At the time there was a young woman evangelist, Miss Ahn Yun Soon, who was assigned to our factory by the Inchun Labor

Mission. She had free access to the mill and even spent periods at labor along with the rest of us. With her assistance we were able to help a lot of the girls. Sickness is very frequent. Miss Ahn enlisted the help of our Christian Hospital in the city and many of the girls were able to get treatment they needed.

On Saturdays either before or after work Miss Ahn and I visited all the Christian girls we knew and reminded them that the next day was Sunday. Then on Sunday we went around gathering up the girls to go to church. We made it a game and frequently after services we would sit in the church and sing and play and talk. On the last Sunday of each month, we held a special Textile Workers' Hour at the church. We had worship and games and discussion about factory problems. If the weather was good we would go on a hike or climb a mountain or have a picnic. The Christmas parties we got up were big events. Almost a hundred girls attended. We sang and played and shared a glass of tea and some cookies. There developed between us a real camaraderie. I am older than most of the others and so I began to find that I was in the role of older sister. I can feel the loneliness and lostness of these kids. I know how important it is for them to have a faith in Christ. They suffer a lot, and are burdened too much. They are hardly more than children. We talk together and search together. About ten of us have regular practice of meeting and talking about the problems of faith. In the midst of this fellowship, I discovered a great change had taken place in me. In our mill there is always an atmosphere of mutual distrust and suspicion. I was as involved in it as anyone. My new discovery was that among lost, lonely girls it is rather senseless to hate someone and fight her when probably her attacks were caused by her own insecurity and loneliness. I began to have the victory of Christ over the situation in which I am involved.

There are many problems that block my attempts to be faithful to my commission. Keeping the sabbath is one of them. Not to go to work on Sunday means back-biting and poor relations with my foreman and fellow workers. To go to work means being sharply criticized by the church people. I need to go to church. I get encouragement and strength and meaning for my life there. Yet the pressures to work are tremendous.

Another problem that constantly plagues me is fatigue. Frequently I am so tired that it is not easy to laugh or show concern for other people. I have all I can manage to get myself through the day. When I feel like this, of course, I am tense and lose sight of my calling.

But perhaps the hardest burden of all is the dissention among the Christians. Even some of the Christian girls in the factory attack me and others for being busy-bodies and non-Christians. There is much to do for the Lord, but we who call ourselves by His name only fight. The people at church say that going to church is God's work, and that the business of industrial evangelism that I am involved in is worthless. In the midst of these troubles Miss Ahn left the factory to be married. Now I am alone. How do I talk to the girls who go to the fortune tellers? How do I visit the girls in other sections when the foremen dislike it? Where do I get the funds to help the girls who are sick? And how am I to bring peace to the sisters in Christ? I am alone and my commission as a "factory apostle" hangs very heavy. If only I had a sister with the same feeling!

Report #3 by Yo Whan Yong

The patterns of relationships between employer and employee are not easily discernible. The situation is too new and the varieties too numerous to provide patterns upon which one can generalize. Nevertheless, there are frequent recurrences of certain problems that make the attempt to isolate and identify them worthwhile. In the following case several of these reoccuring actions are vividly portrayed. Korea is only about three generations into the modern age, and two of these generations were spent under the Japanese oppressors. The relationships inherited both from the old pre-Japanese feudal order and the Japanese imperialism days are still very much a factor in the fabric and emotions of relationships between social classes. Despite the fact that today's factories are worlds apart from the days of feudalism, the inherited concepts and roles are retained. Not only does the employer frequently consider himself as "father" and "benefactor" of his employee, but he also feels his word is law and should not be trifled with by those receiving his "favors." Similarly, the employee often accepts this role of the employer and assumes for himself the part of the loyal son. But as we shall see in this case, workers, while half-way submitting to the employer's domination, are also searching and pressuring for a new role and a new image of themselves. The physical surroundings of a factory, the concentration of men who share ideas and gripes, and the access to new ideas about labor and living standards all work to instill within the workers a demand for change.

A company can make its weight felt in a variety of ways. In October of 1965 when new union officers were to be elected, the plant manager called in a few foremen and suggested that Pak Chae Whon would be a good man for the job. The company could negotiate with the union if they had a man like Pak. The company being rather small with only about 500 employees, the manager's "suggestion" was soon known by everyone. Also because of the size of the shop, the company could fairly easily determine who had taken the "suggestion" and who had not. This time, however, the workers had a different idea. By a large majority we elected Yun Hung Chae to be president of the union. The company backed man was put in as vice president, a position of no authority or prestige.

Then a series of unusual events took place. Kim Hong Hie was one of the men who obviously had not paid heed to the manager's suggestion as communicated by the foreman. One night he was found sleeping on the job. It was not an unusual practice for workers to take catnaps on this shift when work was slow. This time, however, Kim was called on it, and was ordered to write a letter of apology. In our shop reprimands given to workers take the form of making the worker write a letter of responsibility and apology for the wrong he has committed. Three such reprimands cost a man his job. Kim wrote the apology, but nevertheless three days later the foreman told him he had better resign his job. Sleeping on the job was not to be tolerated.

The second incident took place soon after. It had been the custom of the company to give a small bonus in the fall to help the workers prepare their winter kimchi. (Kimchi is a cabbage and turnip type of salad that Koreans prepare in large quantities for the winter when vegetables are not available.) This year the amount granted was about half that given the year before. Rumor had it that if Pak Chae Whon had been elected as union president he could have secured a larger bonus.

The third incident also occurred on the night shift. Lee Ok was a gang leader and an officer in the union. During the lunch break one of the men in Lee's gang produced a bottle of wine. It was his birthday and he wanted to celebrate the day with his buddies. There was enough for one small glass apiece. Just as they were about to drink, in walked one of the company guards. He wrote them all up for drinking on the job. Lee Ok was not present at the time, and had not drunk any of the wine, but being the gang leader, he had to take responsibility. The company demanded his resignation both from the union and as gang leader. In actual fact this meant he was to be dismissed from the company. (Custom dictates that the man in charge in whatever capacity is completely responsible for whatever his subordinates do. If they are caught doing wrong, more than the individuals involved, the immediate supervisor is made to resign. If the crime is big enough a whole line of supervisors' heads may fall even though they were in no way involved.)

It had not been the habit of the company to pick up every little thing as they were now doing. The union tried to stand up for Kim and Lee, but to no avail. The company would not relent. The union president then made the inevitable gesture and offered to resign because he had not been able to save the jobs for the two men. When Lee Ok heard this, in order to block the resignation of the union president, immediately he resigned from his job and position in the union. He tacked his resignation on the bulletin board and formally submitted it to the company. He had fled from North Korea by himself and had

been married for only one month. He had no one to fall back
on, and jobs are not easy to find.

All of this took place within a month after the union election. In November our work contract expired. The union requested a meeting of the Labor-Management Committee to
begin negotiations. (The national labor law requires each plant
to form a labor-management council to solve plant problems. In
most cases these committees are very ineffective and come into
play only during the brief periods of contract and wage negotiations, and even then the committees are frequently bypassed by
private negotiations between one or two representatives of
both sides.) The company's response was, "Let's meet at the
plant manager's house and talk things over." Formal negotiations were avoided and the union set no deadline. A month
passed. Now in December the problem was further complicated
by the end of the year bonus issue. Each December a bonus
equal to one month's wages is given. This year it was in question. Even though the bonus was stipulated in the contract, it
was not always automatically forthcoming. And this year the
old contract was now invalid and no new one had been signed.
The company refused to negotiate on the bonus or the contract.

In the midst of this confusion Pak Chae Whon, the company's choice for union president, began a campaign to undermine the union officials. He bragged that if he were the head
of the union he could get the bonus, settle the contract and, in
addition, get a wage increase. It had its effect. When the workers' representatives met, the union officers were asked to submit their resignations because of their inability to negotiate
with the company. (The union's main body is the workers' representatives who are elected from each section of the plant.
These then elect the president. The president in turn appoints
his own officers.) The men in the plant were dissatisfied and
bitter about the bonus and contract problems. Pak's counter
campaign finally pushed the workers' representatives into the
place where action of some kind had to be taken. The union
officers resigned and Pak was installed as the new president.
Negotiations were opened with the company, but almost im-

mediately Pak found himself in trouble. The company wanted Pak because they figured he would say "yes" to whatever they proposed.

Pak, however, was not quite that obliging. He had been a worker for a long time and had to live among the other men in the shop. He could not be completely subservient to the company. Negotiations hit a snag and seemed likely to break down. One evening, Pak came to my house. I considered him a traitor. He had sold us all out just to blow his own horn, and I wanted nothing to do with him. I wouldn't even invite him into my house. He pleaded for me to help him. He wanted to talk with Yun Hong Chae and to get his support in the negotiations. I had been a union officer in Yun's cabinet. I figured Pak could go stew in his own juice, so I told him to go to hell, but as I said the words, I remembered that I was a member of the Coupling Club. Our purpose was to bring reconciliation. Here I was faced with a case of reconciliation that I would just as soon forget. I relented and promised to talk to Yun. Yun's reaction was the same as mine, "let him fry." But by this time I had come to the opinion that though Pak deserved to fry, the rest of us were in the same fire, and cooperating with him was the only way we could help ourselves. I urged Yun to talk to him. Finally he said he would. The two got together, but Yun could not bring himself to become an active supporter of Pak. During the negotiations Pak came to me and asked about how to proceed in the bargaining. He had no idea of what it was all about. Actually the leadership of the union reverted back to us who had just a few weeks before been asked to resign. Pak, however, maintained for himself the role of head negotiator. The union lost and lost badly. The situation had deteriorated so much that even with Yun's support no one trusted Pak or would have much to do with him. The company, knowing this, pushed him into a corner. There he meekly signed a new agreement. The bonus was cut down to half of what it had been. The contract itself was extended for only three months. And though there was a slight wage increase, the company retained the right of determining how the increase was to be distributed. The company men were rewarded, the others penalized.

We were beaten and demoralized. It was not only because of Pak. The same results may have occurred even under Yun. We wasted our money and efforts in trying to get help from the company or the police or the government agencies, but there is no one really on our side. And we had neither the strength nor wisdom to be able to cope with our own problems. Is Christ really for the likes of us? Does he, and those who are called by his name, have any message, any comfort or action to show us?

3

TAKING SIDES

In 1961 when we first started the UIM ministry, our theology was mainly oriented toward individual factory workers. We hoped that they would be persuaded to believe in Jesus and come to the Christian Church. After several years, however, we became acutely aware that the individual dimensions of belief and church attendance alone were a very inadequate gospel for Inchun's factories. There was no way that the individual could be compartmentalized from the factory system. Nor could the personal, impersonal, and "depersonal" sides of factory life be neatly separated. A worker's individuality and corporateness are integral in his self. They can never be isolated from one another. A ministry that attempts to focus only on the "individual" not only ignores the social self but also distorts a man's individuality.

Our first response to the awareness of these corporate dimensions was to adopt a self-image as a "reconciler." We tried to identify ourselves as those who brought cooperation and reconciliation between management and labor. By acting as a neutral, objective party, perhaps we could help both sides cooperate and thus improve work conditions and labor management relations. Problems could be solved rationally, and everyone would be happy. Such a posture, moreover, was a highly acceptable "Christian" position. We could be the messengers of peace, and as middlemen we could also avoid the areas of conflict.

The flirtation with "reconciliation" did not last long. The facts of life quickly disabused us of the idea. In a society which is basically authoritarian, and where the strength of the workers and employers is so out of balance, for the church (or UIM) to attempt to act as a reconciler would be to help perpetuate a cruel and unjust situation.

There are, of course, unavoidable sufferings inherent in the process of economic development, but the needless sufferings foisted upon Korea's workers by an oppressive, tradition-bound employer class is so pervasive that the words "reconciliation" and "cooperation" have become devices of deception. A Christian missioner has no choice but to set his basic orientation against this class system. He takes sides for the human dignity of workers and against the oppression of the economic-political elitists who run Korean society.

A particular conflict within church circles illustrates the point. In 1970 the East Asia Christian Council gave money to build a "labor center" in the middle of the Inchun industrial area where we had been working for ten years. We opposed the project. Its sponsors were the owner of a large plywood factory and a Presbyterian minister, whom the company hired to act as an assistant manager in charge of health and welfare. The minister held prayer meetings inside the factory and made pastoral visits to some of the workers' homes as well as carrying on his managerial duties. Unfortunately, this factory was infamous for its bad personnel policies, its low wages, and its company-dominated union. About these matters, of course, the minister said nothing.

He and the factory owner, an elder of the Presbyterian Church, did, however, decide they should set up a "labor center" outside the factory in order to carry the gospel to the other workers of the city. To construct a "labor center" in the name of the church with that type of backing was, we felt, a violation of Christian witness. It declared the church to be on the side of the company, and it stood as a direct contradiction to our attempts to stand with the factory workers of that area.

Once in hot debate over the "labor center" issue, a supporter of the project made this attack: "From the point of view of the laborer, your position that the church has to be on the side of the worker may be right, but from the point of view of management, it is wrong. Everyone has his own point of view. Your way is not the only one. You do it your way and let Rev. Lee (the company minister) do it his way. Why do you have to feel yours is the only way? We all have the same purpose of preaching the gospel."

These words raise two major issues confronting Christian mission: First, is everyone equally right in whatever posture he takes? Second, is "preaching the gospel" the one great common purpose that levels everything else out to mere problems of method?

These two problems are questions of theological orientation. The answers which are given in effect define both the content of the message and manner by which that message is expressed. In effect the question is this: Is there any standard by which industrial missioners should decide their posture or position in society? We were claiming that one should stand declared on the side of the poor and the workers. Rev. Lee and his supporters say it is alright to be on that side, or on the company's side, or even in the middle. Everyone has his different way of going about it. Right at the beginning, however, it must be understood that the question must not be defined as strictly a matter of individual inclinations or techniques. It is a question of Christology.

The Jesus we see in the Gospels was a poor man, born of poor parents. He probably worked as a carpenter. He knew fishing and farming. As a member of the lower classes he lived his whole life in their fellowship. Because of his potential as an agitator of the masses, or a revolutionist, the high and mighty of his day, the politicians and the rich, found him to be a threat and killed him. Throughout the whole of his life he lived as a common man of the lower class, and though he had associations with the rich and the rulers, there is no record that he ever tried to become anything other than an ordinary common man. This Jesus is standard for us. He clearly defines our social position and posture. Indeed, it can be said that the incarnation of God took place on this common everyday level of society, and that incarnation is even in our own day fulfilling and realizing itself amongst the poor and the suffering of our world. Therefore, our posture must be in solidarity with Christ's incarnation taking place even today on the docks and in the workshops of Korea. None of our staff is poor as Jesus was poor, but we take as one of our disciplines to become a worker, to live and be among and with them. This is an entirely different attitude from someone who would attempt to preach to the worker or to the poor as though they were the "unfortunates" of society. Jesus' life is clear on this score. He did not move about on earth as a philanthropist or a high positioned person trying to gather merit by serving the poor. He *was* poor.

Recent history teaches us a similar lesson. The scourge of the church has been two concepts: "class consciousness" and "religion is the opiate of the people." When religion plays at being Christian by preaching to the poor while at the same time maintaining its high and lofty security among the rich and employers of society, it becomes a deception to the people. But this deception does not go undiscovered. Class mentality of people sees through it and rejects it. Korean workers have a sharp sense of class position. The minister in the employ of the company may have all the sincerity and good intentions of a saint, but he is seen first and last as the representative of the company. He is a company man trying to use religion for the company's benefit. The rather sophisticated mental manipulations that allow the more highly educated to build up images of religion as something good for the workers become nonsense when confronted with the mundane question of "who pays the guy?" One cannot serve two masters. A decision must be made. It is impossible in the tense, sensitive relations between Korean employers and employees to stand on the employers' side and try to preach Christ to the workers. Scripture and history teach us that the acceptable posture is that of participating in the incarnation through standing with the workers, the poor, the common man of society.

It would not, however, be correct to conclude that Christ is only for the poor and not the rich, only for the laborer and not the manager. Jesus was also for the Pharisees, the rich and powerful of his day. He did not hate them or ignore them. Neither did he join them. He was from birth and intent one of the common poor. His truth and gospel were as true for the rich as they were for the poor. Because Jesus lived and died as one of society's rejects, he has brought hope and salvation to millions of his fellow men. Because Jesus lived and spoke not only in love but also in conflict with the powerful, they also participated in Christ's hope. It is for their salvation that Christ directs his sharpest words and even condemnations against them. The presence of the Christ among the poor gives the strong a necessary witness to humility and humanity. It is Christ's barbs that guide the powerful into understanding the necessity to establish justice, for justice is as necessary for the salvation of the rich as it is for the poor. In our day Christ is on the same side, working for the redemption of the rich.

It is frequently stated that we in the Mission to Labor and Industry are one-sided and narrow. We should, it is said, give more cooperation to owners and management. But such arguments completely misinterpret our posture. We are not anti-management. In Christ you are not anti-anyone. You are pro-everyone. But in order to be for the managers, we must, as it were, stand against them as regards to their inordinate power vis á vis the employee. In order to check and even clarify the issues of human and corporate sin, it is necessary that the witness of Christ among his poor brethren be given. It is a posture of "being against" for the purpose of redemption. In many cases we have stood with unions in disputes against their companies. This does not make us enemies. Because our relationships are channeled through the unions and workers there is the potential for some creativity of response. There are times and issues over which we may be in hot contention with a company, but it is as much for them as for the worker.

It is said that everyone has his own way of going at things. Therefore, those involved in industrial mission should recognize any approach as legitimate. Such statements ignore the historical and social Jesus. They attempt to reduce Jesus to a few general principles that make it easy for everyone. But Christ is not a principle. He is a poor man. To use his name in preaching to the poor while standing in the class of the rich is indeed a grotesque manipulation.

Having answered the first question the way I have, the answer to the second question as to whether "the preaching of the gospel" is the one all-inclusive common purpose, is obviously "no." Is everyone who is engaged in what is called urban-industrial mission joined together in one great fraternity of preaching the gospel? Obviously not. The meaning and intent of that phrase, "preaching the gospel," will vary according to theological and sociological orientation of the missioners. For Rev. Lee in his factory, as well as for many others, "preaching the gospel" can be defined as serving the poor and building up the church. The former is philanthropy and the latter an exercise in adding and subtracting numbers. The assumption is that though the church may be a little short on technique and method, it is still basically sound and holy. It is also assumed that the church contains Christ and his message. The only problem lies in getting that message to the world so that it will accept our church and our Christ. The preached gospel therefore maintains the institutional church and its members as the containers of Christ's redemption. Individually and corporately, the world of industry and men find the answer to their problems by joining with the churchmen. Some men of this persuasion, such as the factory minister, are active in "going out to the world," believing that by changing technique the gulf between the church and men can be overcome.

Whether one "goes out" or "stays in" is, of course, not the issue. The issue is where do you locate Christ and the church? The Christ we see in Scripture lives and dies among the weak of society as one of them. The church in as far as it is his body participates in this same life. A denomination or local organization of Christians are not by some mysterious, automated process transformed into Christ's body. The organizations called by the various denominational names have no inherent, immutable right to identify themselves as Christ's body. Much of the reality and force of Christ's life and teachings have been reduced to formalities and formulas. There is nothing inevitably blessed in reciting prayers or performing the same ritual week after week. And there is nothing eternally blessed about the repetition of phrases, or of acts of charity. The gospel and the Christ must be rediscovered in each age and generation. For us today when the ages have merged into one rapid process of change, it means perpetual pilgrimage. The plight of Korean Christianity is that it still clings to its "Christ" of fifty years ago, and has not yet heard of the Christ of today. It has become static whereas Christ is constantly in motion. "Preaching the gospel" becomes an experience in frustration and frequently an anachronistic expression of class interest.

"Preaching of the gospel," however, should in the first place not be preaching at all. It is discovery, experimentation, and involvement. The gospel may not change, but the reality and vitality of it is revealed over and over again in the world where Christ lives and suffers. The main concern of those who would "preach the gospel" is to discover and participate in Christ. It is in this participating search that the concepts of social justice and individual salvation begin to take on meaning and urgency. It is among the out-manned and over-powered peoples of the poor and working classes that the search is carried on, but carried on not as an academic research project but in solidarity with them as they seek to achieve a greater level of respect for themselves. The search for Christ takes place within a labor dispute where the workers attempt to express their own humanity through participating in the decisions that determine their lives. It takes place in a movement to bring some degree of political rights to a nation's populace. In a word, it is within the search for justice, and the efforts to establish justice in society that Christ is found. "Preaching the gospel" by an isolated church or by a company-paid chaplain is really void of content, because it is not willing to involve itself in the issues of social justice wherein Christ is acting.

The same conclusion is drawn in regards to individual salvation. There are forces that would tend to ignore or even deny the individual's experience of salvation, but on the other hand there is nothing in so-called modern society or modern man which absolutely excludes a man from having a personal experience of relationship with Christ. Modern man can and does meet Christ, but the experience is not limited to an inside-the-church revival experience. It is often channeled through an in-the-world experience of seeking what is true and just in terms of concrete life.

The gospel of Christ is one of social-personal salvation. The individual worker's need for a personal tie with Jesus is as great today as ever, but that personal salvation is located within the action that seeks for justice and social equality. Personal salvation and social justice are not mutually exclusive, nor are they the reverse sides of the same coin. They are integral parts one of the other. A personal relation with Christ is per se a tie to all men and all social problems. Involvement in social action is per se involvement in the person of Jesus and therefore the personalities of the people involved in that social action. Christ's incarnation is not fragmented into compartments. It is a whole body.

Within a period of eight or nine years industrial mission's understanding of itself was transfigured from an individual "churchism" to that of trying to be a "reconciler," and finally to the theology of "taking sides." Inside the act of taking the side of the workers and the poor does the incarnation and our social-individual salvation become revealed.

An Act of Taking Sides

In 1966 the staff of the Inchun UIM asked me to work as a factory pastor to Inchun's one steel mill. Rev. Cho Sung Hyuk knew the president of the union at the steel mill, so he and I paid him a visit.

In Korea the union office is inside the plant. The company provides the office space. Usually it is a small dingy room in some inconspicious, out-of-the-way place. Here, however, the

room was of fair size and located immediately in front of the
company offices. Everything is dirty and dingy including the
company's building. Mr. Chang, the president of the steel workers' local, must weigh about 130 pounds. He stands perhaps five
feet, three or four inches. When speaking his shoulders and
head are bent over and he peers at you out of the top of his eyes.
He gave us a warm welcome, and after Rev. Cho had explained
what we wanted, without hesitation he promised to cooperate
and help me get to know the men in the shop, and would even
introduce me to the union officials and foremen on the floor so
that I could visit with freedom. We discovered later than Chang
had been raised in a very strict Methodist home, where attendance at 5:30 A.M. prayer meetings was demanded every day.
Being somewhat rebellious by nature, Chang resisted the early
rising and the strict discipline of his parents. His stubbornness
earned him the title of *ma-guie,* devil. Finally as a young man
he was put out of the family. His mother said the devil had
possessed him. On his own he had gone to college. Afterwards
he worked for the Democratic Republican Party. From there he
moved over to the Steel Company and within a year was the
president of the labor union.

Beginning with April 11, 1967, every Thursday afternoon
the union president and I made rounds from department to
department inside the mill. His intention was to introduce me
to the union representatives and officers in the plant. In this he
was quite obliging to me, but at the same time it gave him an
occasion to go into the shop. Actually he knew very few of the
men. Not being a laborer himself and having been in the company for such a brief time, he had almost no relationships with
his own union members. In addition, the traditional detached
and formal relations between the high and the low, the ruler
and the ruled, or the leader and the follower, still create
enough mental blocks that the union leader did not feel free
and relaxed among his own men. So in a sense Chang was using
me in order to get himself into the shop. This made us even
since I was using him for the same purpose. He seemed to be
as self-conscious and awkward as I was.

The men in each section elect their own union representative in a manner similar to the way American workers elect their stewards. However, in the Korean situation the representatives do not act as stewards, but actually take the place of a general meeting. They elect the officers and pass on budgets and decide on dispute or strike issues. There were thirty-two representatives. Chang introduced me to every one of them. As we met each of these men it became evident that ninety percent or more were young men who had not been in the factory more than a few years. Chang denied that he had had anything to do with this, but it seems rather suspicious. Of course, it may be that the older men were so fed up with the union that they were willing to let the young guys take over, but in all probability Chang had somehow picked his men.

Having been brought up in Pittsburgh, I knew steel mills were dirty, hot places, but the heat, grime, and danger of this mill are unforgettable. In the midst of a wage dispute that took place in 1969 the company complained that wages were increasing faster than production. I inquired why it was that machines and processes established thirty years ago by the Japanese have not been improved. How could production be increased with such machinery? The answer, of course, was obvious. To change the production process for steel amounts to establishing a whole new plant. It cannot be done piecemeal or one machine at a time. Such a large outlay of capital was impossible, so they had to do the best they could with what they had. Economically speaking, the owners may have been correct, but this did not lighten the load of the workers nor clean the air that they have to breathe. A developing nation is continually faced with the conflict between the demands for investment capital and the demands for immediate relief of human suffering. Nowhere is it seen any clearer than in this steel mill. But, of course, the lack of capital is not the whole story. In talking with the men who work the open hearth furnace, I was told that a process of injecting oxygen into the hot furnace had recently been installed. Before this process was introduced, once every eight hours the furnace had been charged and poured, but now it could be done twice in the eight hour period. This, of course, means stepped-up work for the men within their eight hour shifts. There was, however, no increase in compensation to reward the increased work. The result is a frustrated work force that feels that it has been abused by the company. Part of the difficulties of a developing nation is the lack of capital, but perhaps even a larger part of the problem is the inability, or unwillingness, of management circles to accept the human factor as significant in the production process.

One of the problems that constantly plagued the union was its poor internal solidarity. In talking with Chang and some of the other union men, one of them asked if we at the UIM would help them put together an education program for the rank and file members in the plant. We, of course, readily agreed. This was the exact kind of request that we were hoping to receive. Our UIM staff had been involved in labor education since 1965 and realized how important it was for the rank and file to become more active in their union. This particular request for an education program had an additional significance in that it was part of the union's preparation for upcoming negotiations with the company on a new wage and work contract. Few unions had enough foresight to prepare their members for negotiations by involving them in a preparatory education program. We at the UIM cooperated with the union officers in order to set up a program that they thought would do the union members the most good. "Skills for Union Administration" and "Power in Bargaining" became the two foci of the classes that were held at our UIM offices. The classes were scheduled to fit the swing shift system that the men were working.

Chang showed himself to be resourceful in another way also. He bought a few stocks in the company. When the yearly stockholders meeting was held, he not only received all the company's reports, he also sat in on some of the fighting that took place inside company circles. With this material in hand, he then approached us to help him in preparing for the forthcoming negotiations.

Sung Hyuk suggested that someone with more expert knowledge would be of more value, and if Chang agreed, he would approach a couple of university professors to help us on the job. Chang agreed gladly and thus began a very rigorous month and a half when the union men, the professors, and Sung Hyuk spent hours and hours, often working all night long, checking and analyzing the materials Chang had brought. To our knowledge this was the first time in the history of labor negotiations in Korea that the union had used expert help outside its own organizations. A document was drafted pointing out certain company problem areas. Wage costs was not one of the areas, the professors contended. Wages were low, so that management could not include high wage costs as part of their problems. A wage increase of 40% was demanded.

At the first meeting Chang presented the prepared document. The company was outraged. "Outsiders" had instigated this trouble. Such matters as negotiations were a "family" matter between the company and its employees. An apology was demanded. There would be no further negotiations until an apology was made and the "outsiders" stopped meddling. After this initial meeting, we had supper together with the union men and the professors. The professors advised that the union was on sound grounds.

The next morning there were three unexpected visitors to the office—the factory manager, a department head, and a Mr. Pak, the man whom the union men had gone to see the night before. We knew all of these men quite well. The department head was a Methodist and friend for several years. Pak, I had come to know in the shop as the company's paymaster. Choe, the factory manager, was straightforward. Rumors had it that the union's case was actually being engineered by the UIM. He wanted to know what our role was and why a religious organization should be involved in company affairs. Sung Hyuk was equally direct in his answer. From a Christian point of view, any question of human relations and human problems was a religious problem. In an industrial society one of the most fundamental human problems is that of the relation between a company and its employees. Therefore, our Mission tries to cooperate with the company and union as they struggle to find solutions to their problems. In this particular case the union had asked us for help and so we had introduced them to two university professors. The initiative and leadership was with the union. Our cooperation was in response to their request. Rev. Cho went on to explain that this was actually a big step forward both for the company and union since they could study and discuss matters in a mature way if the union was interested enough to search out the facts of the company. The factory manager's reply was, "That might be so if it were done just by 'our' union men, but what if the outsiders have a strange philosophy? [This is a common reference to Communism.] Outsiders could control the union and ruin the company." "Obviously," he went on, "Chang does not even understand the demands that he is making. He could not answer the questions put to him. It is all someone else's work. Most of the men in the shop do not agree with the way Chang is operating. We do not like outsiders interfering in our business." They suggested that we could help the whole situation by advising Chang to cooperate with the company.

All attempts by the union to begin negotiations were rebuffed by the company. Interference by outsiders would have to be discontinued, they said, before there could be any negotiations. The union backed off and withdrew the documents supplied by the professors. But the union did not back down from making its demand for a wage increase. When negotiations were delayed and no settlement was forthcoming, the men took a strike vote. Ninety three percent voted in favor of strike action.

The company president called for a meeting with Chang in order to avoid a strike. He also requested that Rev. Cho Sung Hyuk join the meeting. Sung Hyuk at first declined, but when the union men also asked him to be there, he consented. Five men met at a hotel in Seoul the day before the scheduled strike: the company president, the factory manager, Chang, the union president, the union's vice president, and Rev. Cho.

The company began things by offering a twelve percent wage increase. The union rejected it as inadequate. Prices were going up between twenty and thirty percent. The ability of the company to pay, worker productivity, overtime, fringe benefits, and the cost of living were then all thrown into the hopper and bargaining began. Before long, however, the temper of the plant manager began to snap. He was not used to having his employees stand up to him and talk as equals.

"You S.O.B., Chang! I hired you and gave you a job. You take our money and still you have the bad manners of talking to us like that!" With that outburst the manager let fly a right hook that caught Chang on the jaw and sent him sprawling on the floor. The manager was a brawny six footer as compared to Chang's skinny five foot three, so there was no response from Chang other than to rub his aching jaw.

The punch on the jaw, however, may have had a cathartic effect, for soon thereafter a package amounting to a twenty percent wage increase was agreed upon and Chang promised to report it back favorably to the union members. The company president then made an unusual confession. He said he was a Christian himself but had never been much concerned about matters of labor relations. Only in the present encounter had he come to see how important such things were. In the future, he said, he would give union affairs his personal attention.

Taking Sides in an American Firm

Tax holidays and a variety of other inducements are given to American and Japanese firms that invest in Korea, but probably the biggest attraction to foreign business is Korea's large supply of cheap, educated labor. Young female labor especially is attractive to industries such as textiles, electronics, and light chemicals. The girls range in age from sixteen to twenty-five. They have an elementary education, work hard and productively, and are willing to accept wages of about thirty to thirty-five dollars a month.

The OAK Electronetics Corporation was an American firm that operated in the Inchun area. It employed about 300 girls, most of whom were farm girls lured to the factory by the hope of earning money. The average wage in 1968 was about seventeen dollars, low even by Korean standards. The American sent over to manage the plant apparently had little understanding of his workers, for he immediately established for himself the image of a tyrant. And as foreign companies frequently do, OAK put a Korean man in charge of personnel relations. He followed the authoritarian pattern set by the American manager. The result was tension and bitterness among the employees. Into this situation came the Metal Workers' Union.

Under the leadership of several men and women inside the shop, a local of the Metal Workers' Union was organized. The company refused to recognize the union. Instead it dismissed the man who had been elected as the union president, Kang Chang Il, charging that he had used fifty sheets of company paper, worth some twenty cents, for his own personal purposes. The union countered by registering a dispute with the government's Labor Committee, and waited out the twenty day cooling off period as the law required. Three days before the end of the cooling off period, after the company manager refused all attempts at negotiations, the home office, located in northern Illinois, decided to send a troubleshooter over to Korea.

It was at this juncture that we at UIM became involved. The district organizer came to our office. He asked Cho Sung Hyuk to talk at a mass meeting of the workers, many of whom were Christians. He then told us that the union had received word that Mr. Bradshaw from the home office was to arrive in a couple of days. He was asking that the union representatives meet with him. The union organizer asked if I would act as interpreter for the union men when they met with Bradshaw. Both Sung Hyuk and I agreed to cooperate.

The meeting with Bradshaw took place at ten o'clock in the morning of October 23. He was apparently pushing for a quick solution to the problem. He admitted past managerial mistakes and on the spot reinstated Kang, with back pay for all the time he lost. The union had a strike deadline for the next day and so put on pressure for an immediate solution not only to Kang's

problem but also to the wage increase demand and the signing
of a collective contract. The company man pleaded that he
needed more time. The proposed contract had not been tran-
slated into English. Bradshaw had shown good faith in reinstating Kang, and his attitude was one of friendly cooperation, so
the union agreed to postpone the strike for a week. Nevertheless, there was much to do and negotiate, so the union suggested a meeting for the next day. Bradshaw not only agreed,
but suggested that the meeting be held in the union's offices in
Seoul. Probably this was the first time in Korean history that
an employer was willing to go to the union's offices for anything. The union men were encouraged.

The next afternoon Bradshaw's attitude had changed.
With cool curtness he announced that the company had decided to close up operations in Korea. The reasons given were
high costs of production, need for larger scale investment than
the company was willing to make, and problems of transportation. He stood up and began to leave. His way to the door passed
me. We shook hands and I expressed regret at this turn in
affairs when things had begun so well the day before. He responded to the effect that the company had to be able to control
its labor costs if it were to see a profit. "But in your talk right
now you said nothing about labor costs." "I thought you would
be smart enough to understand what I meant," he continued.
His voice was full of sarcasm. He went on to ask what religion
had to do with labor problems. I explained that the church had
always been very much involved in all social issues and it was
not unusual for us to help out in areas of human need. "Well,
I'm sure you've had an interesting career!" was his final shot
and out he went. That was the last we saw of him.

It was not, however, the last we heard of him. The company
kept their word and pulled out. The obvious reason for the
withdrawal was a case of bad management, but in order to
cover their path, they passed the buck to the unions, claiming
that the big reason for their pullout was high wages and irre-
sponsible unions. Several international publications quoted
Bradshaw's attacks on the unions. Why he did this we will

never know. Just why he had such a radical transformation in twenty-four hours, we cannot even guess, but one thing for certain is that he and his company, in complete disregard of Korean law, had never entered into negotiations with the unions. He could have controlled his labor costs by the very common method of negotiating them with the union. The Korean government, of course, did not like to lose investors and the company's attacks hit the government's biggest selling point to foreign capital, namely low wages. The company's anti-union blasts had considerable influence on government policy. Within a few months new laws that strictly regulated the operation of unions in foreign invested firms were promulgated by the Korean government.

Foreign firms tend to have the same authoritarian attitude toward labor as do Korean businesses, but the foreigners are in a position to exert even greater political pressure because they control the capital and technology that Korea needs for its economic development. The human rights of the workers, as well as their legal rights to organize and act collectively, are crushed under the arrogance of the foreign and the domestic capitalists.

In this environment we at UIM took sides with the workers. By 1971, ten years after UIM began, we were in close communion with thousands of workers and hundreds of union leaders. We had helped the rank and file union members to participate within their unions, and had given assistance to unions all over the area when they needed help in labor education or in negotiations with the employers. Through all of this, and because of all of this, we were made aware of the power of faith in Jesus of Nazareth. His spirit was drawing us deeper into the factory and personal lives of the men and women of Inchun, many of whom were themselves receiving a witness to Christ for the very first time in their lives.

1971 was also the year I was to leave Korea for furlough back to the United States. Once every five years we missionaries return to our home country to report to the American churches and further our education. The timing for my fur-

lough in 1971 seemed providential. It removed me from the
scene at the very time that the leadership in the UIM ministry
should have passed out of my hands into the hands of my
younger, Korean colleagues. In Inchun we had Cho Sung Hyuk,
Cho Wha Soon, and Yu Hong Shik, and a few miles away in
Seoul there was Cho Je Song, Kim Kyung Nak, and Ahn
Kwang Soo. They are all capable and unusually committed
people. I had no worries about leadership for the UIM ministry.
I resigned from the Inchum UIM and returned to the United
States. Our future was uncertain, but that is normal for a
missionary. We decided to go to the University of Wisconsin to
finish off my doctor's degree in industrial relations and wait
until the Lord gave us the next clue as to what He wanted us
to do.

4

THE **YUSHIN** SYSTEM

The years we were in the United States (1971–1973) were critical and even disastrous years for Korea. During the 1960's Korea had been unique among the non-Communist, poor nations of the world: it achieved a sustained, high rate of economic growth under a relatively democratic form of government. The people of Korea elected their president and chose their national assemblymen. The legislative branch of government had some authority and the judicial sector had some independence. Basic human rights were guaranteed in the constitution. In the 1960's a democratic institution of government, press, labor, and school were going to help to create a decade of economic development.

I do not mean that Korea was a model democracy. There has always been a strong stream of authoritarianism. Even during the 1960's when democratic processes seemed to be in the ascendency, authoritarianism was not far below the surface. In a sense that is what made Korea of the 1960's such an exhilarating place: there was the potential to create something new. Perhaps a democratic society could be established where previously there had been only authoritarianism. Park Chung Hee himself had encouraged the people's dreams of a democracy by governing for eight years under the democratic constitution adopted in 1963. He promised his people he would defend that constitution, but when it came time for him to step aside after two terms as president, as required by the constitution, he reneged on that promise. In order to delay his departure from power, in 1969, he forced through an amendment which allowed him to run for a third term. He promised, however, that he would retire after the third term if the people would elect him again.

His promises were empty. Many people knew that unless Park were stopped in his bid for a third term that there would be no way of ever getting him out. The elections of 1971 would determine whether democracy was to live or die in Korea. Unlike the elections of 1963 and 1967, the 1971 campaign was characterized by open and massive interference by the government police and national guard.

Knowing that Park was mustering every weapon he could think of, the opposition political groups for the first time united behind one candidate: Kim Tae Jung. He was not a well known figure at first, but his gift of dramatic oratory coupled with a clear honesty about the issue of democracy versus dictatorship quickly won Kim a national reputation.

Huge amounts of foreign capital poured in to support Park. Japanese money appeared to be present in large quantities, but probably the largest single gift to Park came from Mr. Robert Dorsey, the President of Gulf Oil Company, which contributed four million dollars.

Park won the election, but not by much. Despite the government interference and corruption, Kim Tae Jung won forty-six percent of the popular vote. If only four percent of the votes had gone the other way, Park would have been beaten. If Gulf Oil had had the decency to keep its money out of Korean politics, Korean democracy might still be alive. In 1971 the Korean people clearly wanted Park out, but Gulf Oil snatched that opportunity away from them.

The election was in May. Six months later Park declared a state of emergency. There was no explanation as to what the emergency was. Park apparently had determined to rid himself of all the limitations put on him by democracy and never again to submit to the humiliation of having to run against an opponent in a national election. The 1971 state of emergency was extended into a state of martial law in 1972. The democratic constitution of 1963 was abolished and Park seized complete and unlimited power.

Under the intimidation of armed soldiers and battle-ready tanks, Park forced the people to vote for a new constitution. This new constitution of October, 1972, called the *Yushin Constitution,* is the exact opposite of the 1963 constitution. It is unlimited, one-man rule. The legislative branch is made a farce. Citizen participation is nullified. Human rights are eliminated. Society, and the very lives of the people, are made dependent upon Park who is free to rule as he wishes. To enforce his decrees, Park uses a ruthless secret police organization called the Korean Central Intelligence Agency (KCIA).

Why has Park done this? He says the dictatorship set up by the *Yushin Constitution* is good for the country: it provides a defense against the Communist North; facilitates negotiations with the North over re-unification of the nation; and speeds up the process of economic development. Each of these three arguments is related to very vital issues within Korean society. Defense against the North is accepted as having absolute priority by everyone. Even the greatest opponents of Park agree that there can be no letdown in guarding against the threat from the North. Korea, however, has been successfully defending itself against North Korea for the last twenty years. No *Yushin Constitution* has been needed in all of that time.

The South has received, and continues to receive, massive amounts of American military aid—some $6.5 billion with approximately $160 million being added each year.

"In as far as military capabilities are concerned, the South Koreans have a significant edge," says a 1974 report from the Center for Defense Information in Washington, D.C. Koreans and Americans agree that there must be adequate defense against a possible Northern invasion. This has been provided for without Park's *Yushin,* or his dictatorship.

Indeed, in 1968 when North Korean commandos slipped into the South and attempted to assassinate Park, there was no declaration of emergency; throughout the whole "Pueblo Incident" civil rights were not suspended; and in the 1960's when hundreds of South Korean soldiers were killed or wounded each year in skirmishes along the demilitarized zone, Park never once declared martial law. In 1972, however, when these threats and tensions had largely decreased, Park claimed he had to establish a dictatorship to defend against the North.

Park knows the Korean people fear the Communists. He plays on that fear in order to build himself up as the only true defender of the people. Park uses a censored press, the police, and especially the KCIA to stigmatize all opposition as Communists, or "fellow travelers." He attempts to instill into the people the fear that there are Communists all around them and only he can protect them. A people who are afraid, he thinks, are more docile, more obedient.

He has found, however, that his people do not scare easily. They know full well the dangers of Communism, but they also are intelligent enough to know when they are being deceived. Park's machinations to use the genuine fears of Communism for his own personal gain only alienate the people and create distrust and disunity within society. Such action on the part of the government weakens rather than strengthens the people's determination to resist the Communists. Surely, even Park should have learned that from the debacle of Vietnam.

A second rationale given for the *Yushin* system is that it gives Park the necessary strength to negotiate with the North on questions of unification. On July 4, 1972 both North and South issued statements that they were willing to begin talks in order to seek ways toward eventual re-unification. Four months later the Park government declared martial law and forced through the *Yushin Constitution* saying that Park had to have the same authority in the South as Kim Il Song has in the North in order to negotiate with him on an equal footing. Everyone knows that Kim Il Song is a Communist dictator. Park says he must be that same type of dictator in order to bring about unification.

Yushin, however, has not resulted in any progress toward unification. Almost immediately after the *Yushin* system was established, negotiations with the North broke down, and are now at a bitter standstill. The "Theological Declaration of Korean Christians" written in 1973 by ministers of several Protestant denominations respond to the *Yushin* approach to unification in these words: "The present regimes in the South and North are using the unification talks only to preserve their own power. They are betraying the true aspirations of the people for the unification of their land." This judgment, I believe, fairly reflects the Korean people's attitude toward Park's pretensions at seeking unification. Two hard-nosed dictators are hardly likely to negotiate with one another.

The third reason given in defense of the *Yushin* system is that it is necessary in order to achieve economic development. This argument, too, is a resort to deception. Everyone agrees that economic development is urgent, but that does not mean that a *Yushin* system is the way to achieve that goal. Indeed, for the decade between 1963 and 1972, before *Yushin*, Korea experienced an economic growth that some have called a miracle. Dictatorship is not a prerequisite to economic growth. Harrassment and suppression of labor do not result in greater levels of productivity. The experience of the Korean economy under the comparatively free system of the 1960's clearly refutes the claim that a *Yushin* dictator is the only way to achieve economic development.

If, then, the three arguments given by the government do not explain the *Yushin* system, what does? Why did Park resort to such extremes? The reason I think is very uncomplicated. Park is a military general. The exercise of absolute power is apparently the chief goal in his military set of values. Furthermore, exercising absolute political power is very lucrative to him and other military men. Greed for power and wealth is the fundamental motivation behind the *Yushin* system.

The establishment of a dictatorship such as Park's *Yushin* begins with the greed for power, but, of course, there must be more than greed. There must be sufficient support for the would-be dictator to allow him to maintain control of political power. In the case of Korea, this support comes from four sources. First, Park did have a considerable reservoir of good will among the people. During his first two terms as president (1963–1971) the people had achieved some improvement in their livelihood and hopes for the future had been created. Since 1971, however, this reservoir has gone dry. Park can no longer rely on the support of the people in order to retain his position. That support must come from other sources.

The army is Park's most immediate source of support. It numbers some 600,000 men who are well supplied with American military equipment. The military also seems to control the police, the riot police, and the KCIA. The KCIA is a semi-military outfit with an estimated 100,000 to 300,000 agents working for it. American military equipment sent for the Korean army seems to have ways of getting into the hands of all of these police groups. In addition, the military has expanded its authority into Korean business establishments. Park can now count on military men in many sectors of the economy to come to his assistance.

The military in all these various aspects appears to be firmly behind Park. Without their support his stay in office would be brief indeed. But without Park, where would all the ex-generals and ex-colonels now in high-paying civilian posts be? Not long after President Gerald Ford visited Korea in November, 1974, the Korean people were treated to the unusual experience of being threatened by the military leaders of their own nation. Meeting at the presidential mansion, the military men declared they would crush any opposition to Park whether that opposition was external or internal.

A third source of strength for Park is the Japanese government and Japanese capitalists. Since the mid-60's, the Americans have adopted a policy of promoting the primacy of Japanese interests in Korea. American pressures led to the normalization of political relations between Korea and Japan in 1965. Since then, Japanese influence in Korea has become dominant. Indeed, one of the chief reasons that the Americans now give for their support of the Park regime is the defense of

Japan. Korea is being defended not for the sake of Korea, but for the sake of Japan. This fact explains why both the United States and Japan are in such close support of Park. They think he is the best hope for Japan.

Park is known to be a man heavily influenced by Japanese ways. He was one of the few Korean military men to be educated at the Japanese military academy during the colonial period. Some say he is more Japanese than even the Japanese. Older Korean people remark that Park's *Yushin* system is like a replay of the Japanese colonial system that ruled Korea until 1945. In Park, the Japanese appear to have a very willing ally.

Japanese capitalists are also playing a large role inside Korea. Since the 1965 normalization of relations, Japanese capital has flooded into Korea. By the middle of 1973 private Japanese investment amounted to $305 million, or sixty percent of all investment.[1] In 1974 the Japanese share increased even further. Many of the Japanese industries are polluting industries, and in many of these work conditions are miserable; but the Park government, in its frenzy to obtain Japanese capital, establishes few standards to control this new form of colonialism.

Finally, Park has the support of the Americans. The military is supported directly by military assistance and indirectly through funds derived from the PL 480 program. American business in Korea, especially the big oil companies, find Korea very lucrative. *Business Week* magazine quotes a Seoul banker as saying that Skelly Oil and Swift and Co. have "in their first year remitted more than they invested. They are cleaning up."[2] Profits for all oil firms have been great. Gulf Oil's gift of four million dollars to President Park can be seen as a token of the American company's appreciation for its good business in Korea.

American AID money is also used to the benefit of Park and his ruling group. AID is in principle, of course, for the building up of the nation. Don Barlett, Pulitzer Prize winner of the *Philadelphia Inquirer,* sums up the AID program in Korea in the following words:

What . . . State Department officials neglect to mention are the oppressive working conditions and an industrial base heavily dependent on cheap female labor and private profiteering and corruption that are so pervasive in Korea that businesses budget for their bribery payments.

Nor do they talk about the major beneficiaries of American foreign aid: a select group of government officials; private businesses controlled by wealthy Korean families; companies run by one-time government leaders or ex-Army generals and joint enterprises managed by Koreans in partnership with Japanese and American companies.[3]

Despite the fact that an oppressive dictator has taken over in a friendly nation, American business continues to make big profits and the Korean elite get rich; the American military feels secure and the Korean military expands its domination over the Korean people. Secretary of State Kissinger was reported to have said that military assistance to Korea has nothing to do with internal events that have arisen in that country. The internal events referred to are the events of a military dictatorship, KCIA harrassment and torture, kangeroo military courts, censorship of all news media, and interference in religious freedoms. The military aid given to Park's army helps make all this possible. Society has been militarized and the American military aid supports the entire military system. Despite Mr. Kissinger's plea of non-involvement, American military aid has everything to do with the internal events that have arisen in Korea.

Park's system of government is called *Yushin*. It is a system not unlike the Japanese colonial system. Even the word *Yushin* is borrowed from Japan and suggest Japanese imperialism. It is the same word used in Japanese history to refer to the *restoration* of the Meiji Emperor to full political authority over the central government and the nation. Park euphemistically translates *Yushin* to mean *revitalizing reform,* rather than *restoration,* but in fact, Park's *Yushin* is a *restoration* of, or a reversion to, colonial authoritarianism.

5
THE **YUSHIN** SYSTEM
IN ACTION

The *Yushin* system, as it has unfolded over the last several
years, has had two major characteristics: rule by presidential
decree and enforcement of those decrees by the Korean Central
Intelligence Agency (KCIA). Law or legal procedure are of no
consequence. Park Chung Hee and his KCIA determine what
is and what is not "legal." They decide who shall and who shall
not be prosecuted, or threatened with prosecution. Hahm
Pyung Choon, Korean ambassador to the United States, wrote
in his book, *Korean Political Tradition and Law,* that tradi-
tionally law was not seen as being for the protection of the
people, but rather it was used as an instrument for the benefit
of the ruling elite. Such a description was never more true than
it is today. Park and the KCIA determine what is law and they
apply it in order to destroy their opposition. Men like Ambassador Hahm, after having received their education in America's
best universities, join Park's ruling elite and espouse his *Yushin* system of government.

The Korean people, however, have reacted to the *Yushin*
in a very untraditional manner. As soon as the martial law
decree of October, 1972 was lifted, they began to struggle
against the *Yushin Constitution.* By the end of 1973 the opposition had gained considerable strength. Thirty leading civic and
religious men announced a campaign to secure one million
signatures calling for the restoration of the democratic constitution. Park must have known that the campaign would have

succeeded, for in order to block it, he issued his first "emergency decree," making it an offense punishable by fifteen years in prison for anyone to criticize or advocate any change in the *Yushin Constitution.*

This decree was announced on January 8, 1974. Nine days later a group of eleven Christian clergymen put their seals to a statement calling for revision of the *Yushin Constitution* in order to restore democracy. They were promptly arrested and sentenced by military court martial to terms of ten to fifteen years.

Two months later university students all over the nation rose in protest against Park and his *Yushin.* Another decree was promulgated. This time Park decreed that it was a crime punishable by death for students to refuse to attend class, or join in demonstrations, discussions, rallies, or any other type of political activity. He further decreed that any other person who might join with a student in any of these actions would also be liable to the death sentence. This decree was then applied retroactively to the students who had demonstrated earlier in the same day and to professors and others who had ever openly opposed *Yushin.*

Professor Kim Chan Kook was Dean of the School of Theology of Yunsec University. On New Year's day of 1974 he had talked to his students about the *Yushin* system. As is the custom in Korea, students visit their professors on January 1st to give special greetings for the new year. Professor Kim explained to his students the dangers of a system that put all authority into the hands of one military general. Three months later he was arrested for having violated Park's decree (issued April 3, 1974) making it a crime to join with students in acting against the *Yushin* system. Professor Kim was tried by the military courts, which Park had established through another decree, and sentenced to ten years in prison.

The Case of the People's Revolutionary Party

About one month after the student demonstrations against Park, early in May, the Korean CIA announced to the nation that it had cracked a huge Communist conspiracy to overthrow the government by bloody revolution and establish in its place a Communist government headed by peasants and the proletariat. This conspiracy, it was alleged, was headed up by an organization called the People's Revolutionary Party (PRP). This party had been able to manipulate thousands of students, dozens of clergymen, and many other top leaders of Korean society. This plot, the KCIA claimed, had originated in North Korea. Two young Japanese men, who at the time were in Korea, were to relay money and arms from the North to the conspirators inside Korea.

Thousands were arrested. Between two and three hundred were subsequently sentenced by the kangeroo military courts to long prison terms. These included the whole staff of the Student Christian Federation, many university students, several Protestant clergymen, Bishop Chi Hak Soon of the Catholic Church, and Yun Po Sun, former president of the Republic of Korea. The two Japanese were given twenty years. Eight men, the alleged ringleaders of the PRP, were sentenced to die.

Under *Yushin* it is not necessary for the KCIA to supply any evidence to support its accusations. Was there any evidence that a People's Revolutionary Party ever existed? How could eight unknown, non-Christian men manipulate university students and Christian clergymen? How were the two Japanese to get enough guns into Korea to defeat Korea's 600,000 man army and its hordes of police and KCIA agents? How could anyone overthrow a government through "bloody revolution" if they had only $6,000 at their disposal as the KCIA reported in the paper? Under *Yushin* it is not necessary to answer such questions. All the KCIA has to do is make accusations. By definition their accusations are the truth.

There are, however, certain formalities that have to be attended to. The eight men, accused of being the ringleaders of the conspiracy, had to confess to their crime and a signed confession from each one had to be presented to the military judge. It is the job of the KCIA to get the confessions. This they accomplish through interrogation and, if necessary, torture.

Interrogation is not a process of sorting out truth from false-hood, it is the technique of getting the person being interro-gated to confess to the crimes that the interrogator says he committed. It is not always easy to know when interrogation ends and torture begins. Are verbal harangues interrogation or torture? Under which category do you put threats against your family and children? Is a systematic attack of lies, deceits, and promises to be accepted as ordinary methods of interrogation? And what about light beatings? When the interrogator's booted foot kicks your shin bone each time a "wrong" answer is given is that torture or just mistreatment? And what about the lack of sleep? Keeping a person from sleeping for a few days does not seem so barbarous until you are the one being forced to stay awake.

And, of course, the Korean CIA makes use of the more strenuous techniques of the trade: cold water is forced through the nose; hot pepper water is poured in the nose of men hanging upside down; electric shock is applied to various points on the body; or perhaps the body is turned in circles at high speeds at the same time that shock is administered. Suh Sung, a student of Seoul National University, appeared in court badly burned. His ears and eyelids had disappeared and his fingers adhered together. He had been "interrogated" by the KCIA.

When the eight men charged with being the ringleaders of the Communist conspiracy were brought to court, there was a signed confession from each. Court procedures allowed each man to make a brief statement on his own behalf. Each one told of frightful tortures and claimed his innocence. Mr. Woo Hong Sun pleaded with the judge to examine the signature on the confession. Even after having been tortured, Mr. Woo had refused to sign a confession. Finally, out of desperation, his captor seized Woo's hand and forced him to sign the statement. If the judge had only looked at the handwriting and compared it with Woo's own writing, he could have verified Woo's inno-cence, but the judge refused to do so. Woo's plea was rejected. Within a very few minutes all eight men were sentenced to death by military generals appointed by Park Chung Hee to act as judges. No evidence had been given, but with the signed confessions in hand no evidence was necessary.

The wives of these eight men were permitted to witness their husbands' trials. KCIA agents had warned them to keep silence. Most of the women, like their husbands, were unsophisticated people. They did as they were told. The shock of the trials, however, woke them up. The military courts were such a farce that even these simple women began to feel their husbands' danger. They began to look for help, and in so doing they turned to the church. I believe it shall always be recorded to the honor of the Church of Korea that it accepted these women. They were not Christians; their husbands were accused of the most heinous crime, that of being Communists, and yet the Christians embraced them as sisters. To be kind to the family of one accused of being a Communist is to put your own life and reputation on the line. Seldom have Christians expressed greater compassion.

The Korean CIA, however, was not happy about these acts of Christian compassion. They warned the Christians to have nothing to do with the wives of "Communists." A directive from the KCIA even forbade the Christians to pray for the eight men or their families. That directive was read at prayer meetings and immediately ignored.

The wives were picked up by the KCIA. At first the KCIA tried their previous techniques of pleading with the women to be quiet—for the sake of their husbands. "The more noise you make, the harder it will be on your husbands," they were told, but the women had been lied to too much; they refused to buckle under. Then the KCIA men switched to the methods they know best. They threatened. They intimidated. They smacked and they beat. After the very lives of her children had been threatened, one woman confessed that her husband was indeed a Communist after all. Then they let her go. She went home and tried to commit suicide by swallowing rat poison. Only the unexpected visit of a neighbor saved her life.

Many people realized from the beginning that the so-called PRP case was a hoax. The KCIA set these eight men up as

Communists in order to try to stigmatize students, churches, and civil leaders as Communists or Communist sympathizers. The whole PRP case was probably a concoction of the KCIA. Rev. Han Kyung Jik of Seoul's famed Young Nak Presbyterian Church joined with Cardinal Stephen Kim of the Catholic Church and fifteen other leading clergymen and lawyers asking President Park to grant these eight men a public, civil trial according to normal Korean legal procedure in order to determine their guilt. Park ignored their pleas.

Finally on April 8, 1975, the so-called supreme court of Korea in a brief ten minute session, without any prisoner or lawyer present, upheld the sentence of death. The next morning the wives of the condemned men were told to come to the prison to see their husbands. They were outside the prison gates waiting to get in when they heard by loud speaker the radio announcement that their husbands had been hanged at four o'clock that morning.

Not once in the year since they had been arrested were they allowed to visit with their wives; lawyers found it all but impossible to defend them; and then less than a day after the supreme court's decision they were all secretly hanged. And to add to the barbarism of it all, some of the bodies were cremated without the consent of the families. Mrs. Song Sing Jin secured the corpse of her husband only to have riot police intercept the funeral, steal the body, and take it to the crematorium while she and her daughter lay crying in the street.

Why were these men murdered in such a fashion? Why were the wives constantly threatened and deceived? Why were the bodies burned? Perhaps no one will ever know for sure, but that is the *Yushin* way. One man demands that his orders be obeyed. Then he turns over the execution of those orders to an unscrupulous, semi-military organization called the KCIA. The result is government by gangsterism. The KCIA probably framed those eight men in order to get at Park's real opposition: the students, Christian clergymen, and other leaders of society. Probably those eight men were hanged secretly so that no one could talk with them and learn the truth. Maybe their bodies were burned to hide the fact that they had been hideously tortured. No one can know for sure, but those are the generally accepted rumors about the case.

Park Chung Hee could have saved those men. Cardinal Stephen Kim, one of the most respected men of Korea, pleaded with Park to intervene. Indeed the eight men had a legal right to presidential appeal, but they were killed before they could make that appeal. Cardinal Kim sent a personal message to Park Chung Hee asking clemency. The message was carried by Lee Hyu Sang, the head of the Democratic Republican Party, Park's own ruling party. Lee reports that after Park had read the message, he laughed and said, "This time we'll scare the hell out of them all." The hideousness of the murder of these eight men has indeed sent fear throughout the whole land. That is the *Yushin* system.

Tonga Ilbo's Fight for Freedom

The story of the *Tonga Ilbo* newspaper must be one of the most courageous in the annals of journalism. The *Tonga Ilbo* began in 1920 during the days of the Japanese colonial persecution. It has been the symbol of independent, dependable news reporting ever since. The *Yushin* form of government, however, finds it difficult to appreciate truthful reporting of the news, so the *Tonga Ilbo,* along with all the rest of Korea's newspapers, was put under strict KCIA censorship. In November of 1974 a government directive was issued to Korea's newspapers. They were strictly forbidden to report any news whatsoever about (1) demonstrations on university campuses, (2) actions of the Christian Churches critical of *Yushin,* and (3) the quality of the coal briquettes used by Koreans to heat their houses. (People were complaining because too much clay was being added to the coal.)

The writers and reporters of the *Tonga Ilbo* refused to accept the directive and went on strike demanding that KCIA agents be withdrawn from their offices. For two days the *Tonga Ilbo* did not appear on the streets. There were no news broadcasts over the *Tonga Ilbo's* radio network. Then, quite unexpectedly, the KCIA backed off. The agents were withdrawn and the *Tonga Ilbo* was back in print. The KCIA, however, was not finished. A new attack was mounted against the paper. A description of that attack was vividly reported by Don Oberdorfer in the *Washington Post* of January 20, 1975:

> The Dong-A Ilbo, one of the great editorial voices of Asia, is fighting for its life against a phantom enemy, South Korea's secret police.
>
> Beginning in mid-December, major commercial advertisers abruptly cancelled their scheduled ads—first one, then another the next day, then a few more, then a host of concellation notices flooded in. In late December major clients suddenly pulled out of contracts with Dong-A Radio, the paper's electronic subsidiary. By mid-January just about all large firms and countless small ones had withdrawn, reducing advertising revenue by about 60 per cent.
>
> Shamefaced and often-frightened clients told a soon-familiar story. Company officials had been summoned by the Korean Central Intelligence Agency (KCIA) and ordered to stop their business with Dong-A at once. Many were required to sign written statements that they would not advertise in the forbidden media.
>
> The advertising director of a large textile chain is reported to have been severely beaten and the company president verbally reprimanded when their ads did not stop quickly enough. The same treatment was meted out to a cosmetics company ad director and his president. This firm's staff was then used to notify other companies.
>
> Department stores, banks, large consumer goods manufacturing firms such as General Motors Korea (a 50–50 U.S.-Korea joint venture) and Hyundai Motors (a Ford licensee) were early dropouts from the advertising lists. Officials of government ministries were reported in the campaign—a Ministry of Health official spreading word to pharmaceutical houses, a Ministry of Culture man informing motion picture theaters, an Internal Revenue agent visiting a publishing firm. Several small advertisers who telephoned the newspaper to arrange ads called back to cancel within a few minutes, leading the paper to conclude that a tapping-and-reaction team had been assigned to its telephone lines.

About eighty percent of the newspaper and radio's advertisement income was cut off. It appeared that the *Tonga Ilbo* would have to capitulate, but then a most surprising thing occurred. One of Seoul's well-known churches, the Kyungdong Presbyterian Church, bought a full-page ad in the *Tonga Ilbo*. The ad declared support for the *Tonga Ilbo's* fight for freedom and pledged the support of the Kyungdong Church in that struggle. This began a movement that, as far as I know, is unparalleled in the history of journalism. Hundreds and thousands of Korean people began to buy advertisement space in the *Tonga Ilbo*. A taxi driver could only afford a space the size of a man's little finger, but he bought that space and wrote: "I skipped my daily glass of wine to support freedom." A group of nine girls working in a textile mill bought fifteen dollars worth of space and advertised these words: "Better to stand and die than bow your head and live." Korean mine workers in West Germany bought space to say "We support the *Tonga Ilbo's* fight for freedom of the press." A doctor wrote: "A bad doctor kills his patient and a bad government kills the people." And one of the former advertisers who was forced to withdraw his support for the paper anonymously sent in money for an ad which ran, "I put this advertisement in the *Tonga Ilbo* to overcome my personal humiliation."

It was a beautiful thing to see. The Korean people were expressing their demands for freedom through the advertising section of the newspaper. Each edition carried dozens or hundreds of these ads. Circulation boomed. From a regular daily circulation of about 600,000, within three months the circulation of the *Tonga Ilbo* shot up past the 800,000 mark and was moving toward a circulation of one million.

Obviously, Park's government could not let this publication of the people's sentiments continue. Pressure was applied to the owner-publisher, a man who had other business interests as well as the paper. He gave in. Fifteen of the leading writers and reporters were fired. Other employees of the company went into an immediate sit-down strike in support of their dismissed colleagues. Then at 3:00 A.M. on March 17, 1975, the police and a large group of "hoodlums" moved in on the strikers, beat them up, and threw them out of the building. The paper was now in complete captivity. Another battle for Korea's freedom had been lost. The *Tonga Ilbo* continues to publish, but now follows the government line. The people have withdrawn support. Major advertisers have been allowed to return.

The Yushin System in Labor

One of the significant and democratic developments of Korea in the 1960's was the growth of the labor union movement. The constitution of 1963 guaranteed that the nation's workers should have the right to organize, bargain collectively, and act collectively. Government policy throughout most of the decade was in keeping with the constitutional guarantees. Union membership expanded from 150,000 in 1961 to roughly 500,000 by the end of the decade. Collective bargaining was regularly practiced, and industrial workers were beginning to participate in their unions and factory life. There were, of course, many problems and most employers did not welcome union action, but, nevertheless, the government adopted a labor policy that was supportive of unions and collective bargaining.

The *Yushin* system of the 1970's, however, has reversed this policy. Instead of union autonomy and bargaining between the employer and employee, the *Yushin* system establishes KCIA control over unions and government arbitration in matters related to wages or working conditions.

Collective action of any kind by a labor organization is strictly forbidden. Bargaining is still formally retained but now the government's Office of Labor Affairs (OLA) dominates the scene. All agreements must be approved by the OLA, and if a union is courageous enough to push demands against an employer, the union leaders have to assume that their major opponent will be the KCIA rather than the employer himself. Because of the KCIA's harrassment, wage problems are settled "peacefully" without resort to collective bargaining or disputes.

Intimidation and control of union leadership is the Park government's major labor policy of the 1970's. Korean unions are organized into seventeen national, industrial unions. The national unions are formed by local or regional organizations, and the national unions then join to form a nationwide federation of labor called the Federation of Korean Trade Unions (FKTU). The KCIA has now gained control of labor at all three levels of organization: the local, the national-industrial, and the FKTU. An examination of KCIA domination of unions at the FKTU level will be illustrative of how it is done at the lower levels.

In 1973 the FKTU held an annual convention for the purpose of choosing officers for the next three years. Each of the national industrial unions sends delegates to the FKTU convention in proportion to the size of the national union's membership. The presidents of the nationals, of course, have a large say in determining who the FKTU convention delegates will be.

Prior to convention time there was a meeting of the presidents of the seventeen national industrial unions. The unusual part of the meeting was that it was hosted by the KCIA. The union presidents were told that the *Yushin* spirit should also prevail among them. There should be unity and close cooperation. At the convention any discord or confusion should be carefully avoided in order that unionism could play its rightful role in building up the unity of the nation. Therefore, the union men were told that there should be only one candidate for the office of FKTU president. They were also told who that candidate should be.

In order to prevent any misunderstanding as to the intent of the government, each of the union presidents and convention delegates were paid private visits to "explain things."

By the time the convention opened, each of the delegates had been so completely intimidated that for the first time in the history of Korean unionism only one man was nominated for the office of FKTU president. That man was Pai Sang Ho, the choice of the KCIA. Korean labor had been humiliated, but that was the *Yushin* spirit: unite under one ruler even if you are humiliated in doing so.

A year later a revolt erupted on the floor of the FKTU convention. Delegates ignored the presence of KCIA agents and demanded that Pai resign. So great was the uproar that Pai finally promised to resign within three months. This, however, he has not done. The KCIA is not likely to permit him to resign. If he did, it would look like the KCIA was listening to the demands of the people, and if that ever occurred, it could ruin the whole *Yushin* system.

One bizarre footnote must be added. The American AFL-CIO has an agency called the Asia American Free Labor Institute (AAFLI) in Korea. AAFLI has contracted with the FKTU to assist it in labor education and social services. For these activities AAFLI does not use AFL-CIO funds. Rather, it uses generous supplies of money from the American government's AID program. So, in effect, we have the AFL-CIO using money of the American taxpayers to help support the KCIA's hold over the labor movement in Korea. And at the same time that the AFL-CIO is doing that, many American unions, such as those related to textile industries, are trying to get Americans to boycott Korean goods. On one hand the AFL-CIO helps create oppressive working conditions in Korea by its support of FKTU, and at the same time it wants the American people to abolish the Korean workers' jobs by refusing to buy their goods.

If American labor is interested in preserving their jobs, they won't succeed through boycotts. Boycotts will only add to the pressures that workers in the poor nations are now under. In order to compete, labor in the poor nations will be forced to even cheaper levels. American unions should not pit worker against worker. Only through solidarity with workers of the poor nations can American labor help itself. The opponent that must be confronted is not labor of the poor nations, but international business. The AFL-CIO is certainly showing no solidarity to Korean labor. In fact it gives every appearance of having joined business and government against labor in Korea.

Under the *Yushin* system Park Chung Hee issues the de-

crees and the KCIA carries them out. Estimates of KCIA man-
power range from 100,000 to 300,000, many of whom are military men.[1] It is an agency that not only deals in foreign intelligence and protection against the Communist North, but is also
"quite clearly a secret police. It strikes at will, without warning, or warrant, and is beyond the law and the courts."[2]

Nor is the KCIA confined to Korea itself. Kim Tai Jung, the
leading political opponent of the Park regime, was kidnapped
by the KCIA in Tokyo and secretly taken back to Korea. The
pro-South Koreans living in Japan are under the constant tyranny of the KCIA. And in the United States, in every area
where there is a large Korean population, there is also a large
number of KCIA agents. Koreans in the United States are
harrassed and their families in Korea threatened if they (Koreans in the U.S.) dare say anything critical of Park's *Yushin*
system.

Even more blatant have been the efforts of the KCIA,
with the help of the Korean Embassy in Washington, to bribe
American lawmakers. It is estimated that from $500,000
to $1,000,000 per year have been channeled into the United
States to influence legislation concerning South Korea. Ironi-
cally, the original source of these funds is probably the U.S.A.
itself. Park Tong Sun, the Korean businessman who has acted
as the front for the KCIA in these matters, is alleged to have
received large sums of money from his family's ties with Gulf
Oil and from a variety of American grain companies that ship
rice to South Korea.[3]

6

YUSHIN AND THE CHURCH

One of the earliest and most persistent voices of protest against Park's *Yushin* system has been the Christian churches. Christians of Korea number about four million people, or between ten and fifteen percent of the population. They are a Bible-centered, evangelistic group of believers who are staunchly anti-Communists. Christians also have a history of standing against oppression. As early as 1919 they were active in the anti-colonial, independence movement.

On March 1st of that year a non-violent demonstration against Japanese imperialism swept over the Korean peninsula. Of the thirty-three leaders of the campaign, sixteen were Christians—this despite the fact that Christianity (of the Protestant version) had been in Korea for less than thirty-five years. Throughout the colonial period, the Christian church was a center of strong anti-Japanese sentiments, and many of the leading men in the struggle for freedom both abroad and in Korea's internal underground were Christians.

After liberation at the end of the Second World War, a Methodist Christian became president of the southern half of the Korean peninsula. Syngman Rhee had become a hero of legendary proportions by the time he rose to power in 1948. But Rhee was an old man, a man of the nineteenth century. In 1960 he was driven from power by a student uprising because of massive corruption and the cruelty of his police. The student uprising that unseated Rhee was not an anti-Christian movement per se, but it was highly critical of the church and Christianity. Christians, too, felt the embarassment of the situation. The morale of the Christians was never lower than in the days immediately after the fall of Syngman Rhee.

During the 1960's the churches withdrew from involvement in social or political matters. Revivalism again became the chief focus of attention. From its early beginnings the Korean church had been keen on revivals. Two or three mass revivals had swept Korea in the early days, and even to the present most local churches will hold one or two revival meetings a year. The revival experience is intensely emotional. People are put under a seering conviction of sin and they experience the sweet refreshment of the Holy Spirit. The experience is deeply personal, but almost entirely private. In the 1960's much of Korean Christianity withdrew into the shell of revivalism.

Evangelism, in the sense of winning new converts, is an intimate part of the Christian faith for Koreans. In the 1950's Syngman Rhee established a chaplaincy program in the army. Not only were the chaplains of service to the military organization, but the program gave Christian preachers an opportunity to evangelize the soldiers. Many thousands of them responded by being baptized. In the 1960's a comparable arrangement was worked out with the police and the homeguard of veterans on active reserve. Christian ministers were given the opportunity to serve and also preach to tens of thousands of Korean men and women whom they otherwise would have had no way of reaching. The content of the preaching was invariably the private message of personal salvation.

There was, however, a trade-off involved in these various chaplaincy programs. At the same time that the ministers were allowed to preach to the troops, the police, or homeguard, they were also expected to attend meetings or briefings that explained to them government policies and programs. The clergymen then passed on this information to their congregations. During the later years of the 1960's when Park was making his first moves to establish a one-man rule, this channel through the church pastors into the Christian congregations was very important and heavily used.

Yushin and Urban-Industrial Mission

As the 1960's ended and the Park regime moved towards *Yushin,* however, tensions began to develop between the KCIA and the church. The first open expression of the tension between the two occurred in 1970 over the death of a young man named Chun Tae Il.

The building in which Chun Tae Il worked is a block-long, two-story maze of small cubicles euphemistically called "Peace Market." Inside each cubicle, some of which have no more than four or five foot ceilings, young boys and girls work endless hours for a wage amounting to less than thirty dollars a month. Chun Tae Il was twenty-two years old when he died. With a copy of the nation's labor laws in one hand, and a fervent plea for justice for his fellow workers, Chun Tae Il burned himself to death. His flaming body lit up the wretched Peace Market sweat shop and evoked a groan of anguish and protest from workers everywhere in the country. Church pastors immediately began to sermonize on the evils and oppressions that caused the death of this young man; student groups held memorial services; and the government, hoping to prevent the drama of Chun's immolation from erupting into widescale demonstrations, claimed him as a national hero.

Chun Tae Il was a Christian, as are many of the other young workers in Peace Market. Chun's co-workers asked UIM and the Catholic JOC to hold the funeral. A few university students volunteered to assist. The government, however, fearing that Chun Tae Il would become a symbol of working-class resistance, refused to allow the funeral to be held. Instead, the Office of Labor Affairs took over and buried Chun's charred body at state expense. Government officials eulogized Chun as a great patriot declaring that their policies for rapid economic development would prevent the need for others to suffer as Chun had suffered.

The JOC's and UIM protested to the government and the

labor unions about this political use of the boy's body. The government was indignant that any group would dare criticize it, and the unions were so afraid of the government that they reacted in anger. The death and funeral of this young boy became the first in a series of incidents where the UIM people and the JOC's, by attempting to assist a victim of some tragedy, found themselves at loggerheads with government authorities and labor leaders.

A second incident occurred a few months later. A manager of a textile mill in Yongdong-po hired two "goons" to break a union that his employees were forming. The two were given free run of the mill. When Kim Jin Soo, a young man of 21, refused to buckle under threats, one of the two grabbed a screwdriver and drove it into his head. For five hours Kim was left lying in the company manager's office before he was finally taken to the hospital. By then it was too late. Kim Jin Soo died.

The company quickly changed plant managers and claimed no responsibility for the affair. It was, they said, a tragic fight between two individuals and had nothing to do with the company. The National Textile Workers' Union echoed the company's words. The union declared that the death of Kim Jin Soo was unfortunate, but it was brought about by an argument between individuals. His death was unrelated to the union in any way.

The family of Kim Jin Soo and some of his friends came to Rev. Cho Ji Song and Rev. Kim Kyung Nak of UIM for help. These two men immediately went to the Textile Workers' Union to ask for support in getting compensation for Kim's family and in helping to establish a union at the plant. Instead of support, the two ministers got abuse. "Why are you interfering in union affairs?" "Who are you to tell the union what to do?" "Mind your own business!"

The response from government officials was no better. Kim Jin Soo's body lay in the hospital morgue for two weeks because there was no money to bury him. Finally, after a demonstration in front of the morgue by some workers, UIM missioners, and university students, the government put pressure on the company to pay a small compensation so that Kim could be laid to rest.

The relations of Urban-Industrial Mission with government officials and national labor leaders never recovered from the conflict that ignited around the deaths of Chun Tae Il and Kim Jin Soo.

Under the *Yushin* system labor unions came into captivity by the KCIA. At the annual convention of the FKTU in 1973, the union leaders completely surrendered to the KCIA and in the spirit of *Yushin* put forth only one nominee for president. Top union leadership had caved in. Local leaders who still attempted to work for the rights of their union members often found themselves harassed as much by the FKTU as by the KCIA.

The Hankook Mobong Textile Mill is located in Yongdong-po on the west side of Seoul. The company was doing a good business until it was transferred to new management. The new manager's chief qualification to run the business was that he had high political backing from the Blue House. ("Blue House" is a term comparable to the American "White House.") With the help of that Blue House backing he received a large loan from the bank supposedly to help operate the textile mill, but within only a few years that money was gone; the company was in heavy debt; all the funds to cover the employees' severance pay and the total amount of the workers' savings under a national savings program had disappeared. The new owner went into bankruptcy claiming that he was completely destitute.

The bank that had granted the loan to the new manager demanded that the loan be repaid. The company would have to be auctioned off so that the bank could recoup its losses. Anyone who would buy the company, however, the bank authorities maintained, could not be required to repay the workers' severance fund or savings program. This loss the workers would have to bear themselves. In addition, a new owner coming in would have to be free to reorganize the work force as he saw fit. Some workers, even union officers, might have to be dismissed.

The owner with the Blue House backing, the unseen politicians in the deal, and the bank would all end up with a nice profit, and the workers would be left holding the bag. Hankook Mobong, however, had a strong labor union. Solidarity among the workers was unusually well developed. The union opposed the auctioning of the company unless the workers' claims were met. Lay-offs by any new owner were also opposed. Experience at other plants made it quite predictable that the first ones to be laid off would be all the union officers. After that anyone not docile and loyal would also be put out and the new owner would bring in his own people.

On New Year's day of 1974 the acting president of the company invited the union president out for a drink to talk the situation over. The two men got into a company car, but instead of going for a drink, the car was driven to the backyard of a neighboring factory building. There the company president told the union man to get out. As he did so, the chaffeur met him with a solid right hook to the jaw. Then the company president and the chaffeur proceeded to work the union man over. He was found lying on the ground and taken to the hospital. It was two weeks before he was well enough to be discharged.

Again, as in the case of Chun Tae Il and Kim Jin Soo, the FKTU and the National Textile Workers refused to get involved. The president and vice president of the Hankook Mobong local union came to Rev. Kim Kyung Nak, Rev. Ahn Kwan Soo, and Rev. Cho Chi Song of UIM and also to Father Jack Tresillini, leader of the Catholic JOC. After studying the situation, talking with the representatives of the union, management and government, the UIM men and the JOC leaders held a prayer meeting. At the prayer meeting a letter was penned and sent to both the FKTU and the National Textile Workers' Union accusing them of betraying the rights of workers and calling for their resignations if they could not carry out their duty to defend the rights of workers and local unions.

The response of the FKTU was to issue a large, expensive advertisement in all of the big daily newspapers of Seoul. The advertisement accused the industrial missioners of having lost their own calling to holy orders. It said that they (the missioners) were interfering in purely union affairs in order to build up their own political power. The FKTU threatened to crush industrial mission and those involved in it if they did not stay out of union affairs.

Many of the FKTU leaders opposed the publication of the attack on UIM, but the men closest to the KCIA prevailed. In one unpublished statement the KCIA-union leaders accused the UIM of being a Communist-front organization trying to take over the union movement. The absurdity of such an accusation is obvious to everyone, but the government and the KCIA have opted for the absurd position that any and all opposition stems from Communist sources. UIM offices are said to be harboring spies; UIM tactics, they claim, are the same as those used by the Reds; UIM people have a strange ideology; and UIM missioners agitate and cause social disorder. One KCIA agent reported that the "problem of UIM" was so urgent and subversive that it had been placed directly under the jurisdiction of the Blue House. All UIM missioners were to be closely watched.

KCIA surveillance of UIM work intensified. Two examples of the KCIA attack, one in Seoul and one in Inchun, will reflect the general conditions which UIM people have had to endure under the *Yushin*.

In Seoul there is an area on the east side of the city called Chung Kye Chun. It is a seemingly endless row of miserable shacks built on both sides of a city sewage ditch. The stench, the rats, worms, and vermin are not easy to describe. In this Chung Kye Chun area lives a small group of UIM missioners.

Rev. Kim Jin Hong is representative of these men. While still in seminary, he and his wife, a graduate of Ewha University, took their baby and moved into a shack beside the sewage ditch. Kim felt that if Jesus were living in Korea, he would be here living among these people.

Part of the ministry carried on by Rev. and Mrs. Kim was quite conventional. They began a church for worship and a little school for children who had no means for going to public school. The "school" was located in a dark shack that had no floor, but university students from Seoul National University and Ewha University gave voluntarily of their time to teach the children. Rev. Kim also became involved in the healing ministry. The sufferings of the slum people because of sickness and disease are tremendous. In most every family someone is sick. The Chung Kye Chun area, of course, has no hospitals or doctors or nurses. The people have no money for such luxuries. Rev. Kim contacted the Seoul City Hospital and a few private clinics pleading for them to accept charity cases. Though he was not successful in securing the amount of help needed, a few places did promise to cooperate. After that, many of Rev. Kim's days were spent carrying people to the hospital and seeing that they were taken care of. Often he had to carry them on his back. There was no money for other forms of transportation.

Perhaps Kim Jin Hong's most unconventional characteristic was his compassion and his willingness to spend himself for people about whom no one else cared, but the characteristic that made him known to the city authorities was his insistence that the people living in the Chung Kye Chun area had a right to organize themselves into a community. The problems of sanitation are unbelievable, and, without the aid of the city authorities, they cannot possibly be met. Rev. Kim saw that only an organized community could persuade the authorities to act. The city had plans to eventually tear down all of the slums and move the people out of the city. In the meantime they were not prepared to improve the living conditions for fear the people would want to stay. City plans had dragged on and on, however, so that some of the people had already lived beside the sewage ditch for over ten years. The most the government had done was to move out a few pockets of people here and there, and even this was done in such a brutal manner that hundreds of people had suffered the loss of what little possessions they had been able to acquire over the years. Without warning the city fathers would send police in to clear an area. Often as not the locations where the displaced people were sent were nothing but vacant mountain land. Sometimes tents were provided, but often not even that.

Rev. Kim's concept of community and humanity told him that even slum dwellers had rights. These rights could be expressed through community organization and corporate action. Gradually, as he, his wife, and the volunteer workers became accepted in the Chung Kye Chun area, he began to organize men and women around problems of housing sanitation, unemployment, and education.

The city authorities looked at Kim's work with suspicion. He was seen as a meddler and a troublemaker. Kim was supposed to be preaching religion, but instead he was interfering in problems of drinking water, sanitation, and housing. These were not matters of religion. Rev. Kim's operations in Chung Kye Chun, they speculated, must have purposes other than religious. Police and KCIA were sent to keep a close eye on him and his church. The spirit of *Yushin* allows for no initiative, no action outside of that ordered by the political authorities. Rev. Kim was in violation of that spirit and, therefore, had to be kept under surveillance and control.

KCIA interference in Chung Kye Chun mission and its harassment of the missioners and their families and friends led to Kim Jin Hong's arrest. He and ten other young men, convinced that rule by the KCIA could no longer be tolerated, signed a petition demanding the restoration of democratic processes. Rev. Kim was sentenced to fifteen years in prison.

In Inchun the KCIA attack upon the UIM ministry took a different form. In 1973 Rev. Cho Wha Soon took over as head of the Inchun mission that Rev. Cho Sung Hyuk and I had begun in 1961. Cho Wha Soon's first experiences in UIM work were described in chapter 2. During her eight years with UIM she became deeply involved in the personal and factory lives of the young girls who were employed in Inchun's textile mills.

As the KCIA's paranoia with Communism deepened, Rev. Cho's position among the female workers of Inchun came increasingly to their attention. The girls who associated with Rev. Cho and the other members of the Inchun UIM staff were not the meek, retiring girls that the company wanted. They stood up for their rights and frequently knew more about the Labor Standard Act and other labor laws than did the management. Such girls are troublesome for managers who are used to having their words unconditionally obeyed. Such girls arouse the suspicion of the KCIA because girls are not "supposed" to act like that. There must be some Communist agitation somewhere.

On a day in April, 1974, a thousand girls at a wig factory went on strike and refused to work. The company had withheld the severance pay of the girls who left the factory; the company dormitory was dirty and did not come close to meeting the standards set by law; and on several occasions the girls had been hit by their male supervisors. The girls were demanding redress for these three grievances. Until the National Emergency Decree of December, 1971, employer and worker representatives would have met and resolved the girls' complaints, but after 1971 such freedom of action had been eliminated. It became the prerogative of police and KCIA to settle such problems.

Six of the strike leaders were taken to the local police station for questioning. Much to their surprise the police seemed less interested in talking about the strike than they did in talking about Rev. Cho Wha Soon and the Inchun Urban-Industrial Mission (UIM). The girls were warned that Rev. Cho and her co-worker, Choe Yong Hi, could well be Communists. There had been cases, they were told, where Christian ministers had actually worked as Communist spies. Then the police interrogators asked if Rev. Cho or any of the Inchun Mission had any connection with the strike at the wig factory. The girls denied that any connection existed. After exhortations to stay out of trouble, they were released.

A few days later, however, the same girls were again picked up. This time it was by the KCIA who are not as gentle as the police. Two of the girls were beaten until they confessed that they did know Rev. Cho and the Inchun Urban-Industrial Mission. Several of them had in fact attended education classes sponsored by the UIM, and Rev. Cho and Miss Choe had consulted with the girls on the problems of severance pay and dormitory conditions.

A few weeks later there was a picnic. UIM holds picnics twice a year for the industrial workers of Inchun. On this occasion the picnic was only for girls. About 100 attended. Before lunch a worship service was held. Rev. Cho Wha Soon gave the sermon. She spoke on Matthew 6:33, "Seek ye first the kingdom of God, and his righteousness; and all these things shall be added unto you." When it came to explaining "his righteousness," Rev. Cho made reference to the ordeals of the girls at the wig factory and recalled that the police had insinuated that she herself was a Communist because she tried to support the girls in their trouble. She went on to say that in today's society if one tried to lead a righteous life, he might have to give up fifteen years of his life. (A reference to the punishment given clergymen who had defied President Park's Emergency Decree of January 8, 1974.)

The next day (Monday) when the girls went to work, they were summoned to the plant manager's office. Their names had been given to the company by the KCIA. The plant manager told the girls that unless they stayed away from UIM they would all be fired. Forty-one of the girls were later taken by the KCIA and made to write down everything they had heard Rev. Cho say at the picnic.

At 6:00 A.M. on May 15, a black jeep with two men in it pulled up at Rev. Cho Wha Soon's house. She was taken away to the Inchun offices of the KCIA. After four days she was sent to the infamous *Namsan,* Seoul headquarters for Korea's CIA. From there she was transferred to West Gate Prison where she was kept in solitary confinement for three months. No charges or explanations were ever made. Her whereabouts were known to us only through Korea's amazing "grapevine" communication system. After three months, she was released. No charges were made, nor explanations given.

Why was Rev. Cho Wha Soon arrested and then suddenly released without charges being made? The reasons were proba-

bly two. First, it fit into the general pattern of harassment
against the UIM. Secondly, it appears that the KCIA was trying to connect Rev. Cho with an alleged Communist conspiracy
that the KCIA claimed to have broken in April, just a few
weeks before she was arrested. Apparently unable to make a
case against her, they finally let her go. Rev. Cho is now back
in Inchun but under constant surveillance. Police harassment
and threats against the workers have all but eliminated the
formal ministry of the Inchun UIM.

Yushin and the Church

The *Yushin* system was initiated in October of 1972. In
1973 there had been two skirmishes with the Christians. Pastor
Myung Ki Eun of Chun Joo, in the south of the country, had
been arrested for refusing to support the *Yushin Constitution.*
And in Seoul Rev. Park Hyung Kyu and a few young clergymen
had been arrested for allegedly circulating an anti-government
prayer during Easter Sunrise services.

In 1974, however, the conflict erupted into a general confrontation between the Park regime and the Christian
churches. The act igniting this conflict was Park's declaration
of two "emergency decrees" on January 8, 1974. All criticisms
of or attempts to alter the *Yushin Constitution* were made
crimes punishable by fifteen years in prison. And, secondly,
those charged with violating the first decree would be tried by
military courts.

One week later, eleven Christian clergymen including Kim
Jin Hong violated Park's emergency decree. They issued a brief
statement calling for:
1. The withdrawal of the emergency decrees,
2. Free discussion of the *Yushin Constitution,* and
3. The restoration of democratic order to society.

The very fact that Park had issued such emergency decrees
had alerted many people to the type of dictatorship they were
now facing. The act of these eleven clergymen dramatized to
the Christian community the stand that the church had to take
and the price it must be willing to pay. Before they had issued

their statement the ministers knew what the consequences were likely to be. Yet all of them knew that the type of police state and KCIA harassment under which they now lived could not be accepted by Christians. Therefore, they acted.

They were arrested and hauled in front of military courts for sentencing. Each man was duly sentenced to terms of ten to fifteen years. The attitude of many of the Christians was expressed by one of the eleven during the trial. The military judge launched into an attack on preachers: "Why are you here?" he asked. "You are supposed to be religious men who preach the gospel. Why have you left religion and become political agitators?"

The response was, "We are here because we believe in justice and democracy. Why are you here, judge? You are a military general committed to defending us against invasion from the North. Why are you here helping to oppress the people you swore to defend?"

Two months later another decree threatened death to anyone acting against the *Yushin* system. Christian students, the entire staff of the Student Christian Federation, and many clergymen were arrested. These, too, were tried by military courts. When the wives or mothers, who were the only ones allowed in the courtroom, reported the accounts of beatings, tortures, false confessions, and crudeness of the judges, they, too, were arrested by the KCIA, threatened and beaten. The anger of the Christian community began to spread.

At the same time Christians became aware of the fact that plainclothes police and KCIA agents were coming to church gatherings and monitoring what was being said and prayed. Pastors began to be detained for what they said in their sermons. Word drifted up from the southern provinces of how Catholics had been prevented from attending worship services, and church elders were warned that student activities in the churches had better be curtailed.

More than anything else, however, it was the KCIA's charges of Communism that pushed the churches into confrontation with the government. The KCIA declared in May of 1974 that there had been a Communist conspiracy to overthrow the government. It then proceeded to accuse some of Korea's leading Christians, including a Catholic bishop, of having taken part in that conspiracy. It had been common practice for the KCIA to smear UIM missioners with the charge of Communism, but from May of 1974, they widened the attack accusing or insinuating that the church was full of Communists.

Korean Christians have been fighting the Communists for over half a century. Before the Russians occupied North Korea in 1945, most of Korea's Christians lived in the North. Under the tyranny of the Communists, thousands were executed and hundreds of thousands fled to the South. When the North invaded South Korea in 1950, it was apparently the policy of the Communist authorities to round up Christian pastors and elders and shoot them.

Communism for the Korean Christians is a deadly enemy. It is an atheistic force which has militantly sought to eliminate religion and Christianity. For the KCIA to claim that churches and preachers were fellow travelers or had participated in a Communist conspiracy was an outrage. It disparaged not only their patriotism, but also their faith. The KCIA cannot accept the truth that the Christians are working for justice and democracy. It is capable of explaining opposition only in terms of Communism. It is this KCIA obsession with Communism that has more than anything else angered the Korean Christians into protest. Perhaps the Park government thinks it can intimidate the Christians and spread division among them if they call "Communist," but in fact the results have been just the opposite. Of one thing most Korean Christians are confident: their fellow Christians are not Communists. The KCIA attacks have been instrumental in bringing Christians, Protestants and Catholics, into a new-found fellowship with one another.

Response by the Church

The first response by the Christians was a predictable one: they held a prayer meeting. It was a prayer meeting for the men and women imprisoned under President Park's emergency decrees. It was decided to hold the meetings every Thursday morning until the people were released. At first only a few of the family members attended, but as the government attacks increased so did the size of the prayer meetings. By the end of 1974 two or three hundred people were gathering each Thursday. Prayer meetings and Catholic masses for political prisoners became a regular feature of church life, not only on Thursday mornings, but on almost any day of the week somewhere, sometime, some Christian group was holding a prayer service.

As the Christians gathered, so did the KCIA agents and the riot police. If there were a hundred people attending a prayer meeting, you could predict that there would also be a dozen KCIA men and about three hundred riot police, in full battle garb, equipped with tear gas and pepper fog. If the meeting was in Seoul's Myung Dong Catholic Cathedral, where several thousand could gather, there would be several dozens of KCIA men and an army of battle-ready riot police. The Christians never gave any sign of turning the prayer meetings into violence, but the government apparently appreciates the explosive nature of prayers. Overwhelming, intimidating force was sent against each Catholic mass, each Protestant prayer meeting.

From the government's point of view the show of force was perhaps justified, however, for these prayer meetings were not ordinary prayer meetings. They were prayer meetings that wrestled with the Lord about the evils of oppression that have befallen the Korean people. They pray that God will deliver them from the bondage of *Yushin* and bring them into the promised land of freedom and democracy; they pray that the Lord God will abolish that instrument of the devil called the KCIA; they pray that the political prisoners will be given strength to endure; and they pray that Park Chung Hee will repent and believe in God so that he will do what is just.

These are prayers that are given in deep anguish of soul, and they are prayers that are prayed openly, knowing full well that KCIA agents are taking down every word. At the beginning of one meeting a Presbyterian pastor stood up and said, "For my prayer last week I was arrested, and harshly interrogated by the KCIA. If anyone here is not willing to risk similar treatment, perhaps he or she had better leave." No one moved. Many are the people who have, like that pastor, been taken to the KCIA for their prayers.

On one occasion a wife of one of the men condemned to death told about how she had been kept at the KCIA headquarters for several days. They had harangued her, beat her, and threatened the lives of her children. When she told this story, the prayer meeting exploded. The people rose up and grabbed the KCIA agents and threw them out the door.

Two other responses to the government were also made. At the prayer meetings and masses they began to pass resolutions. This, too, has a "churchy" ring to it, but these resolutions have not been vague moral concepts. One representative statement ended with the following six demands:

1. Immediately abolish the *Yushin Constitution* which is trampling on the rights of the people. We demand that representative government by a national parliament be restored.

2. We demand that President Park, who is following the path of a Communist-type dictatorship, step down from the presidency so that a true democracy can be established.

3. Dissolve the Korean Central Intelligence Agency which has silenced the press and the voice of the people, and has oppressed the freedom of individual and group action.

4. We applaud the *Tonga Ilbo's* recent declaration on freedom of the press and demand that KCIA surveillance of the press, schools and religious organizations stop.

5. We oppose the visit of the President of the United States because that visit is an expression of support for the Park regime which does not have the trust of the people of Korea.

6. Immediately release all those who are in prison for opposing the *Yushin Constitution*.

Resolutions with such demands as these were passed at the prayer meetings and masses and then widely distributed. Often the *Tonga Ilbo* newspaper would publish them for the whole nation to see.

The next response of the Christians was as direct and

"churchy" as the others: they put into effect the admonition to love one's neighbor. They opened their fellowship to the wives of the men who had been condemned to death for allegedly being part of the so-called People's Revolutionary Party (PRP). The only place in all the society where a defense of these men could be expressed was in the Christian circles. This expression of Christian love infuriated the KCIA. Prayer meetings and masses were warned that all references to the PRP must be eliminated. Wives of Christians in prison were told that it would go hard on their husbands unless they (the wives) discontinued all relations with the families of the eight condemned men. KCIA threats, however, went unheeded.

Efforts by the Christians for the eight men were of no avail. The men were hanged. Priests, ministers, and Christian laymen protested their murder and comforted the families of the slain men. Many were arrested for these acts of compassion.

One of the women, upon hearing of her husband's death, cursed the Christian God. She had gone to Protestant churches and Catholic masses, but it had been useless. If there indeed was a God, he was weak or cruel. Useless!

A few days later she returned to the Thursday morning prayer meeting. Her rage at God had passed. She realized, she said, that working together in faith was the only way her husband's death could have any meaning. She was welcomed by the tears of fellowship born from common suffering.

Government-KCIA pressures did not have the intended results. Instead of becoming docile and obedient, the Christians became more determined in their opposition. In January of 1974 only eleven Christians took a stand against the *Yushin*. By the end of the year official statements demanding a return to democracy were made by the Catholic Church, the Presbyterian Church in the Republic of Korea, the Methodist Church, and the Presbyterian Church of Korea. These groups account for about seventy percent of the Christians in Korea.

7

MISSIONARY IN 1974

When my family and I left Korea for furlough in 1971, we were uncertain as to whether we would return. I knew that the time had come when I, as a missionary, should absent myself from our Inchun UIM ministry, but I had no leads as to what the next stage of my ministry should be. Professor Everett Kassalow at the University of Wisconsin had encouraged me to complete my doctoral studies in the field of industrial relations, so using our furlough time we returned to Madison.

Madison, Wisconsin, is one of the most beautiful places in the world, but both Dorothy and I were uneasy about taking up permanent residence in the United States. Once one has been a missionary in a land like Korea, much of American life becomes bland and trivial. We really did not want to exchange the depth of life in Korea for the apparent shallowness of the U.S.A., but yet we did not want to return to Korea without a clear calling and a clear mission assignment. It often occurs that we missionaries become so enamored with life in our adopted countries that we continue on even after the specific reason for our presence has ceased to exist. We did not want to end up our missionary life in a vague limbo after we had experienced such depth of involvement in the Inchun situation.

The solution to our dilemma came in a manner that could not be ignored. One Sunday morning at church I was paying no attention to the sermon. Instead I was meditating upon my own future. What to do? Where to go? With a Ph.D. in industrial relations could I return to Korea and teach? If so, I could have access to new areas of mission where no one else had yet been, and at the same time I could help out the friends in UIM without really being in any position of authority. What school would accept me? Yunsei, the Protestant university? SuKang, a Jesuit institution? Song Kyun Kwon? Korea University? What about Seoul National University?

This last idea caught my imagination. Seoul National was by far the best known school in business and commerce. A position there would be stimulating and provide an entrance into Korea's industry. I liked the symbolism of a Christian missionary teaching in a non-church, completely secular university. It would provide opportunity for study and research into industrial relations and give me firsthand contact with the young men who would become Korea's managers of the future. The location and social position of an assignment at Seoul National would be different from that of UIM in Inchun, but using that UIM experience perhaps I could contribute a new dimension into the thinking of the students about labor-management problems.

The idea of teaching at Seoul National stayed with me. I wrote a friend in Korea and shared the idea with him. He called up the dean of the College of Commerce of Seoul National. By pure coincidence, the College of Commerce was itself looking for someone to teach in the field of industrial relations. Within a few weeks I had received an invitation from Seoul National, had sent to them the required documents, and our family's dilemma about the future was resolved. We would return to Korea in the fall of 1973.

We got back to Korea on September 29. My first lecture at the university was three days later. Before we could get far into the course on "Labor's Role in Economic Development," however, the university was closed down. By the end of 1973 the conflict between President Park and the Korean people was already quite serious. University students all over the nation rose in demonstrations against the government. The students, of course, lost, but tensions increased. KCIA agents became more and more visible. Their presence in every sector of society created fear and anger.

Before leaving the United States, I figured that my mission in Korea would probably have three parts: teaching, research, and cooperation with UIM. It soon became apparent that any kind of meaningful research into labor problems would be impossible. There was too much distrust and suspicion brought on by the ever-present KCIA. Teaching was constantly interrupted by student demonstrations and government closures of the university, but, nevertheless, I did continue teaching through my remaining time in Korea. The students at Seoul National are eager to learn and very much interested in labor problems. I taught courses in "Introduction to Labor-Management Problems," "Collective Bargaining," and "Comparative Labor Relations Systems." My stay at Seoul National College of Commerce extended over three semesters, all of which I enjoyed immensely.

The third part of my mission, cooperating with the UIM ministries, took on a character which I had not expected.

One of the first requests for help that came from UIM concerned the case of Hankook Mobong, mentioned in the last chapter. I attended a meeting with the UIM missioners, Father Tresilini of the Catholic JOC's, and the union people. KCIA agents took the names of everyone at the meeting. Earlier when I had visited the union leader in the hospital, five agents had been standing outside the building. As I emerged, they took my name and address. This turned out to be the pattern for all subsequent UIM meetings. The KCIA was always there.

In May of 1974, Rev. Cho Wha Soon was arrested. The KCIA just took her away. She was never charged. Neither her parents nor her bishop were ever informed as to why she was taken or where she was. Rev. Cho and I had been close friends since 1966 when she joined our Inchun UIM staff. She was a genuine sister in the faith. Another missionary and I decided we would visit the KCIA headquarters to see if we could get any news about her.

On a previous occasion I had met a man named Lee Sang

Kyu who was in charge of the religion section at Namsan (KCIA headquarters). We went to the main gate and were met by a soldier with a rifle.

"What do you want?"

"We have come to see Lee Sang Kyu of the religious section."

We were taken to a small office where two more soldiers sat. The first soldier explained our presence.

"There is no one here by the name of Lee Sang Kyu," one of them told me.

"That's funny. I met him here only a few weeks ago, but if he is not here, let us meet with anyone in charge of the religious section."

"You must be in the wrong place, there is no religious section here." As the one soldier said this, the others looked at each other muttering, "religious section?" as though it were the first time they had heard the words.

"We have come to find out about the case of Rev. Cho Wha Soon. We will talk with anyone who is in charge of her case."

The soldiers assured us they knew nothing of such things, but if we would wait, they would call someone.

In a few minutes a young man in a brown leather jacket appeared. "You have come to see someone called Lee Sang Kyu, but there is no one here by that name. Please go now."

"We have come to find out about the case of Rev. Cho Wha Soon. Let us speak with someone in the religious section."

"There is no religious section. Go."

"Why are you playing with us like this? We came to ask an honest question about a friend. Why do you not answer straight? Let us see someone in charge."

"You came to see Lee Sang Kyu. Since he is not here, leave."

"We will not go until we have talked with someone about the case of Rev. Cho Wha Soon."

The leather jacketed man turned and left. Within thirty seconds he was back. "Lee Sang Kyu is at a tearoom across the street. You can see him there."

We went to the tearoom. Lee Sang Kyu assured us he was doing everything he could to save Rev. Cho Wha Soon. He knew her and had great respect for her, he said. When his boss asked for information on Rev. Cho, he had reported many good things about her.

"What are the charges against her?"

"That is not decided yet. We are still investigating."

"But how can you arrest someone and keep them in prison without even notifying her parents as to why she has been arrested?"

"You do not understand our system. She would not have been picked up without some good reason. But put your mind at ease. We are doing everything we can for her."

This meeting was our first with the KCIA, but it taught us two lessons: first, never believe what a KCIA agent tells you, especially if he is a low level man. Lies and truths are inextricably mixed up in everything they say. And secondly, be very careful of agents at the higher levels like Lee Sang Kyu. Lee is a friendly man, a warm man, an intelligent man, who, if you are not careful, will make you think he is on your side. You go away relieved to know that your friend, or husband or son or daughter, is in the hands of good men like Lee Sang Kyu. Only later does it dawn on you that Lee is a deceiver. He has no power. He makes no decisions. He probably knows nothing of the case at all. And in any event your loved one is not in his hands. His suaveness and "goodness" are the cover for evil. The KCIA has many such refined front men.

During the first four months of 1974 about 1,500 people were arrested for political reasons. Of these, somewhere between 200 and 300 were finally sentenced to long prison terms by the kangeroo military courts. Many of these were men whom I had known and worked with for years and years. As the arrests increased and the reports of tortures and sufferings came out, I began to exercise a type of ministry that I had not foreseen. It was a ministry of pastoring to the families and acting as an interpreter for the UIM missioners who were either in prison or under KCIA harassment.

As the Christians went into prison, their families and friends began to meet for prayer. Korean Christians are conservative people with a thorough understanding of the Bible and a firm belief in the power of prayer. Each Thursday morning since May of 1974, they have gathered at the National Council of Churches' building for prayer.

It was in these prayer meetings that I came to know many of the wives of men whom I had known for years. I had met Rev. Kim Kyung Nak's wife before. She had been hesitant when her husband decided to go into UIM work. She is a pretty, soft-spoken woman who could not bear to tell her two children that their daddy would be in prison for fifteen years. To keep up their hopes, as well as her own, she told them that daddy had gone to America. Under the intimidation and threats of the KCIA this once bashful and gentle young lady came to lead demonstrations and face up to battle-trained riot police.

I met for the first time the wife of Kim Jin Hong. After her husband was arrested, she remained in the slums and continued the work she and her husband had started. The church under her leadership had experienced a revival. New believers by the dozens joined the congregation. Five months after her husband was arrested, she gave birth to their second child. That newborn child was laid in a bed that was even more humble than Jesus' manger.

Ahn Jai Woong I had known for a long time, and I had talked with him only a few days before he was arrested. Ahn had been married for only a few months before the KCIA had come for him. I met his wife at the Thursday morning prayer meeting. She is a tall, beautiful girl. She was allowed to be present when her husband was brought before the military courts. When the trial was over, she went directly to a reporter for an American newspaper and told him what had happened: how the trial was a farce without evidence and without defense for the accused. She reported the prisoners' stories of beatings and tortures.

Because she had dared talk of these things to a newspaper reporter, and especially a foreign reporter, Mrs. Ahn was arrested the next day. She was threatened and beaten until she was hysterical and had to be taken to a KCIA hospital. After she regained consciousness, the abuse was begun all over again. When she was finally released, Mrs. Ahn went to the American newspaper reporter and told him exactly what they had done to her.

And I also met Mrs. Pak Hyung Kyu, an older woman whose husband was pastor of First Presbyterian Church. She also is a woman of great courage, and has been a mother to many of the younger wives. And, I will never forget the wife of Lee Hae Hak. She, too, continues the work of her husband among the poor. She can lead the music of a revival meeting, or comfort those who are suffering, and with her children she is love. She and her imprisoned husband exchange letters of moving poetry.

Under the threats of the KCIA, and under the loneliness of being "widows," these women and others have become the vehicles of grace for many people. Among the many blessings that I have received in Korea, the opportunity to know them, and at times to minister to them, has been one of the greatest. There was not much I could do, but I could be a friend and a pastor, and this I attempted to be.

One of the burdens that these women have had to bear is the misunderstanding of some of their fellow Christians. The government has publicly accused their husbands, sons, and daughters of breaking laws and helping the Communists. The prime minister of the nation has claimed that some of the Christian clergymen have apostatized, left their holy orders, and have become political agitators. It is not easy for some Christians to understand what is going on, especially when the prime minister of the nation takes to himself the authority to judge the holy orders of clergymen. What does preaching the gospel have to do with political things? Why are Christian pastors and even a Catholic bishop in prison? The misunderstandings and suspicions about the acts of the imprisoned Christians often were expressed in criticisms against them and their families.

In Korea all church pastors are Koreans, but frequently missionaries are asked to preach. I had opportunity to preach almost every Sunday. I like to preach, and especially to Korean congregations. They are very responsive. During my last year in Korea (1974), each time I spoke, I felt it encumbent upon me to interpret to my listeners just why it was that many of the Christian brothers and sisters were in prison.

It would have been possible for me to forget our common ministry, our life together. I could have claimed immunity on grounds that I was a "professor," or on grounds that I was a "foreigner," but to have done such would have been a denial of my ministry over the last twenty years, as well as a betrayal of what I understand the Christian gospel to be. I sought for and cherished communion with my Korean brethern. Now that they were under persecution their communion meant even more to me. It was important to me and, I believed, to the entire Christian world to understand and accept the witness that these people were making, so I attempted to interpret their actions to Christians in the churches of Korea.

My sermons were not complicated. Usually they would include the following points: (1) Why was Rev. Kim Kyung Nak in prison? He deliberately broke President Park's emergency measure that forbids anyone from criticizing his *Yushin* system.

(2) Why would a Christian pastor do that? There are two reasons. First, Rev. Kim has been a pastor to workers and labor unions for ten years. He has seen workers oppressed, union leaders arrested, and the labor union organization taken into captivity by the KCIA. He himself has been arrested and beaten by the KCIA because of his attempts to serve the workers. The system of government which makes all this possible and gives the KCIA its authority is the *Yushin* system. The emergency decree says no one can criticize this system of rule by the KCIA. Rev. Kim says such a system cannot be accepted by Christians. Secondly, Rev. Kim feels that the citizens of society should have the right to participate in selection of the president and members to national assembly. The *Yushin* sys-

tem takes away the citizens' rights and gives the president complete control of everything. In other words, Rev. Kim believes democracy is better than dictatorship. President Park's emergency decree sets up the dictatorship, therefore Rev. Kim would not recognize that decree.

(3) What does Scripture say about such matters? Scripture teaches us to repent of our sins and believe in Jesus as our savior. Under Rev. Kim's ministry many workers have come to know Jesus as their Lord. Scripture also tells us in Luke 4:18 that we must preach good news to the poor, release to the captives, and freedom for the oppressed. This Rev. Kim has attempted to do in his ministry to the factory people and their labor unions. And Scripture tells us through the prophets of the Old Testament that God demands justice and a social structure where the rights of citizens are protected. Rev. Kim believes in social justice and has spoken out for it. Jesus' gospel is for the salvation of our individual souls and for the salvation of our society. Because Rev. Kim and the others believe in this gospel, they are now in prison.

When in early December the Korean government moved against me to deport me, KCIA agents had records of my sermons. My sermons, they said, were an interference in Korean politics and therefore a violation of my visa.

My sermons are, I replied, not political. I am not politically motivated nor am I in support of any politician or political party. My sermons are a witness to the teachings of Scripture as regards salvation, justice, and human rights.

In August of 1974, another kind of unexpected ministry came my way. My family and I went on a vacation to Taechun Beach, a beautiful place on the Yellow Sea. While there a young friend of ours came to visit. She claimed she was not a Christian, but she certainly did witness Christ to me. "Why was it," she wanted to know, "that Christians prayed for themselves all the time and forgot everyone else?"

That was a mystery I could not explain, but I did ask her what in particular she was talking about.

"Each Thursday you Christians hold prayer meetings for

political prisoners and then all you do is pray and make statements about Christian clergymen, Christian students, Christians, Christians. Don't you realize there are others in jail, too?
Don't you know that there are eight men who are under the
death sentence? They are probably innocent, but they probably
are going to be killed just to cover the tracks of the KCIA about
this so-called Communist conspiracy. Why don't you Christians
pray for those eight men?

She was, of course, absolutely right. Even though I had not
paid much attention to the case of the "People's Revolutionary
Party" (PRP) in which these men were alleged to be involved,
it was generally assumed at the time that the KCIA's charge
of "Communist conspiracy" was falsehood. The KCIA charged
that these eight men had been able to manipulate university
students, Protestant clergymen, a Catholic bishop, and leaders
of Korean society into taking part in a Communist-led revolution. Such a charge was absurd. We knew that the charges of
Communist were a trick of the KCIA to discredit any opposition
to Park Chung Hee. We knew from the students and clergy and
other friends who had been arrested that the accusation of
conspiracy was a pure concoction. Yet we had paid little attention to the eight men who were charged with being the ringleaders of this nonexistent conspiracy.

Our young friend's attack upon us Christians hit the mark.
She was right. I picked up the old newspapers and began to
re-read the KCIA's case against the "People's Revolutionary
Party" (PRP) and the eight men. I was amazed. I had read these
same articles before, but now I read with different eyes. The
entire case was one set of assertions after another with little
attempt to support the assertions with evidence. It was charged
that certain men had contributed large sums of money to support the revolt, yet when I added all the figures together, the
total amount did not exceed $6,000. What kind of a revolution
can you produce with $6,000? How were eight unknown men
with $6,000 going to overthrow a government supported by a
well-armed 600,000 man army? Such questions the KCIA apparently never asked. Or at least they never attempted to answer them.

One evening about a week after we returned from our vacation, I received a phone call. The woman's voice on the other end of the line said she was a friend of Mr. Lee's wife. She wanted to know if she could come to see me about a matter. I could not immediately identify who Mr. Lee was, nor could I know who the person talking was, but since it is always assumed that telephones are tapped, communication is frequently indirect and surreptitious. I asked the woman to come the next morning early before I left to go to the university.

I was unprepared for what happened. Not one woman, but eight women showed up. They were the wives of the men sentenced to death. For two hours I listened to what they had to say. At times it was bedlam—everyone was talking at the same time; I could not understand the *Taegu* accent of Mrs. Ha Chae Won; and Mrs. Lee Sou Byung's baby decided to cry a bit. But the message of the ladies was loud and clear. (We missionaries came to identify these women when speaking to each other as "the ladies." When anyone said "the ladies," we all knew he was talking about the wives of the eight men.) They were sure their husbands were innocent. They gave examples of how the KCIA's charges were false or fabricated. Each of them had been at the military trials where their husbands had been sentenced. Each told of how their husbands had pleaded their innocence. Each of the wives related how their husbands told of being tortured until they signed a confession. Mrs. Woo Hong Sun told how her husband even after electric torture had refused to sign the false confession, but a KCIA agent forcefully took his hand, wrote his name, and then inked his thumbprint to the confession.

Now I was really up against it. The story these women told fit with what we knew had happened in many other trials held by these military courts, and the newspaper reports seemed to substantiate the claim that these eight men were being "set up" by the KCIA. Where did I go from here? It did not take much imagination to realize that the PRP thing was dynamite. It was the very heart of the KCIA's charges of a conspiracy. If these men were innocent, then obviously the KCIA's case against the university students, Christian Student Federation, and clergymen was also a fabrication. What does a Christian, and in this case a missionary, do in such a situation? Does he drop the whole thing because he knows it is likely to bring more trouble than he wants, or does he continue to press on?

I decided to investigate a little bit further and write down what I discovered. What I learned was that a quite similar case had existed in 1964. Three of the accused in 1974 were connected with the 1964 incident, but at that time government charges were shown to be unsubstantiated, and the case dismissed. Indeed, the prosecutors in charge of the case resigned rather than prosecute because there was such a lack of evidence. Even the term "People's Revolutionary Party" (PRP) had been affixed by the government to the group of intellectuals it was trying to prosecute. The term "People's Revolutionary Party" was found to have been a name made up by the KCIA.

The 1964 case was just one more attack of the government against Korea's liberal and progressive political movements. Ever since colonial days Korea's extreme right has attacked and assasinated non-Communist, liberal minded people with the same enthusiasm as it has eliminated Communists. The 1964 case was one more battle in this continuing effort to completely erase independent liberals.

For ten years the men connected with the 1964 case were under close KCIA surveillance. Families, friends, places of work, and financial situations were under constant watch. Then in 1974, just when the Park government needed a reason for silencing its ever growing opposition, the KCIA again brought out the "People's Revolutionary Party" (PRP). Three of the men charged in 1964 and watched ever since were arrested as heading up the PRP. Seventeen others were picked up as being members of the group. They were all middleaged or above. None of them was well known or important. There were no rich people among them. No intellectuals. No Christians. They were unknown outside their small circle of family and friends. Most of them had not even met one another.

Using these eight men, who had no way of defending themselves, the KCIA trumped up a "conspiracy" in order to charge

its constant enemy, Korea's progressive, democratic movement, with having collaborated with the Communists. If the
KCIA could pin the tag of Communist on the students, Christians, the clergymen, and social leaders, they could send many
of them to prison and also alienate them from the sympathy
and support of the Korean people.

I was being taken in a direction that I did not want to go.
The decision to study the situation had now put an even
heavier burden on me. There were only two possible ways to go:
back off or share my findings with others. I did not want to back
off, play the coward and abandon "the ladies," but neither did
I want to go to prison or fall into the hands of the KCIA. I
shared my findings on the case with other people. I wrote it all
out and gave it to some of the church leaders, to a couple of
professors, and other friends. A copy was even taken to the
American Embassy. I was hoping against hope that someone
else would spring to the rescue. No one did.

On October 10, 1974, I spoke at the regular Thursday
morning prayer meeting for political prisoners. Using Matthew
25:31–46 as my text, I said that at times Christ is mediated to
us through the outcasts or oppressed of society. Thus through
the sufferings of our brothers and sisters in prison on political
charges we can see something of the suffering of Christ for our
society. Those who are symbolizing Christ to us, however, are
not only the Christians in prison, but also the non-Christians.
There are eight men who have been given the death sentence.
The KCIA has provided little evidence against these men. They
have probably committed no crime worthy of death. Their sufferings are not only their own, but are the sufferings of our
entire society. Therefore, we Christians should pray for their
lives and their souls.

The next afternoon about 5:00 P.M. two KCIA men came to
our house to take me away. They said I would be gone only for
a couple of hours, but I knew the "couple of hours" was a
standard lie that they told everyone. Since my wife was not
home at the time, I left a message for her saying I had gone to
the "South Mountain," a euphemism for the KCIA headquar-

ters, and that I would be back in a "couple of hours."

The ride to the South Mountain KCIA headquarters was an experience in itself. The driver darted in and out of Seoul's rush-hour traffic like he was on a mission of death. As soon as we arrived at the KCIA place, I was taken to room 306. There were two interrogators waiting for me. Normal Korean manners of introducing oneself and saying something nice were dispensed with. Interrogation began immediately. I was told that I would have to write down every question and answer in Korean, so for the next seventeen hours I practiced my Korean handwriting as I had never practiced before.

"Why do you have prayer meetings on Thursday mornings?"

The answer, of course, they already knew, but I explained how we met to pray for the Christians put in prison under President Park's emergency decrees.

"What right do you have to pray for the release of criminals? The government has judged them guilty of breaking the law. What right do you have to try to get them out of prison through prayer or any other means?" Mr. Huh, the chief interrogator, was indignant. He was the one who was always hostile. Mr. Yun, the other interrogator, played the role of my friend. Once a question was asked, I would give an answer. Then Huh would usually harangue me for the insincerity of my answer. I would answer again. The question would be put again, and somewhere along the line Yun would act as "mediator" so that some acceptable answer could be written down. The answers were to be completely my own free answers I was told, but in fact I could write only after I had been put through the attack by Mr. Huh and his miserable disposition.

"You gave a sermon at the Thursday morning prayer meeting. What did you say?"

"I spoke on Matthew 25:13 urging Christians to pray for the eight men condemned to death since they are the ones suffering the most."

"You said that the men of the People's Revolutionary Party were innocent. You praised and spoke on behalf of the Communists, didn't you?"

I assumed that they had notes on what I had said, which, of course, was a safe assumption since all the Thursday morning prayer meetings were monitored. "I believe I said that the KCIA had presented little evidence against the eight men and that they probably had committed no crime worthy of death. Therefore, we Christians should pray for their lives and souls."

"Such talk is in violation of the anti-Communist law," Huh informed me. "Did you know these men were Communists before you gave your sermon?"

I responded that I knew the KCIA had declared that these men were Communists, but as an individual I did not know whether they were Communists or not. Huh was infuriated. How could I as an individual dare question the judgment of the government? The government had decided! There was nothing more to say. By questioning the government's decision I was insulting the Korean people and their culture.

This was the nub of the matter, and we went over it time and again: What right has an individual to be critical of government decision? I claimed every right. They claimed no right.

After thirty or forty minutes of talk about government and the individual, the questioning took a different direction:

"After you preached, someone prayed. Who was he and what did he pray?"

"His name is Rev. Pak. I do not know his full name. He is, I believe a Presbyterian."

"What did he say?"

"I cannot remember everything, but even if I could, I would not tell you. His words are his responsibility. Anything I say could be used against him."

Mr. Yun assured me that at the KCIA they did not do things like that. Everything I said would be held in strictest confidence. When I remained stubborn and refused to answer, Huh then read off from his notes the prayer that Rev. Pak had given.

"That's what he said wasn't it?"

"You will have to ask him," I replied. I did not know it at the time, but that is exactly what they were doing. Rev. Pak had been arrested just a couple of hours after I had been. Later, when we compared notes, we found that we had been kept in the same building and they had questioned him closely about what I had said in my sermon assuring him that anything he said would be held in the strictest privacy.

Next I had to write down every place I had lived and worked since high school. They questioned me in detail about how I had become a missionary, how I was assigned to UIM work, and how long I intended to stay in Korea. And, of course, they wanted to know the names and addresses of all the people I knew in Korea. I provided the names of friends that I was sure they already knew. I had been told by others who had gone through KCIA interrogation that this giving of names is one of the standard techniques of the KCIA. If, for example, I gave a name of a friend who is not already involved in my case, he is visited by a KCIA agent. The friend is told that I connected him with some illegal act or that I had said that he and I had discussed the case of the "People's Revolutionary Party." This friend is then blackmailed into cooperating with the KCIA and giving testimony against me in order to save his own neck. And in any case, word is spread that I am giving witness against my friends to the KCIA. So when I come out I am alienated and suspect by everyone. In this way the KCIA's enemies are kept fighting against one another.

Around eleven o'clock at night I was taken to the office of Lee Yong Taek, chief in charge of the KCIA's 6th section.

"You have been in Korea a long time, Mr. Ogle, but obviously you still don't know much about Korea. And you know nothing about Communism. You have violated our anti-Communist law, but because you are a foreigner, we are going to be generous. I am going to prove to you that these PRP men are indeed Communists."

Lee then repeated to me the exact same stuff that had come out in the newspaper. He went back to the 1964 case, but added nothing new. The only piece of evidence that he showed me was what he said was a copy of a speech made by Kim Il Song, the Premier of North Korea. One of the eight condemned men, Ha Chae Won, had listened to the North Korean radio and copied down Kim's speech and then showed it to some other people. Otherwise, Lee Yong Taek appeared to have no more support for his case against the so-called PRP than the government had back in 1964 when the case was dismissed.

Then an amazing transformation took place. Instead of a cool, calculating man reciting alleged "facts," Lee switched over into an emotional monologue.

"These men are our enemies. We have got to kill them. This is war. In war even Christians will pull the trigger and kill their enemies. If we don't kill them, they will kill us. We will kill them!"

"If our government does not kill these men, I will go to the national cemetery and confess before the grave of every dead soldier that our country has been sold out to the Communists. I will go to the United States and visit the graves of Americans killed in Korea and I will confess how they have shed their lives in vain. We've got to kill them! We will kill them!"

What was going on? Lee's emotional solioquy certainly could not have sprung out of the "evidence" that he had shown me. His eyes were lighted up and his face expressed real satisfaction with himself. He was on an emotional jag that was beyond me. A few days later, however, I discovered a piece of information that could possibly explain this diatribe. It seems as though he was the man in charge of the 1964 case. When the prosecutors resigned rather than bring the case to court, Lee had suffered a great humiliation. In 1964 there were still democratic legal processes so the KCIA could not force the case through. Now in 1974, this same man, freed of all legal restraints, was having his revenge and paying off for his humiliation. To add to the dimension of personal vendetta, it happens that the district attorney at the time of the 1964 case is now the head of the KCIA. He, too, had personal scores to settle over the 1964 debacle.

Huh, Yun, and I returned to our cubicle. Interrogation was continued, and this time we began on UIM. They wanted to know how it started, who was in it and all the details. By the time that was finished, it was about 1:30 A.M. Huh was getting tired. He instructed Yun to make me write down the names of all the wives or family members of men in prison whom I knew. I was to tell when I had met them and what we had talked about. Huh then stretched out on an army cot and went to sleep.

Yun and I continued on for another two hours even though I would talk only about two or three people whom I was sure the KCIA already knew about.

Before I was allowed to sleep, Yun informed me I would have to write a *kaksuh,* a statement that includes elements of confession of wrongdoing, apology for those wrongdoings, and a promise not to repeat them. Yun and Huh apparently had agreed on the *kaksuh* that I should sign. It had three parts. First, I was to say that "I did not know the PRP men were Communists when I spoke on their behalf"; second, I was to promise that I would obey all government policies; and third, I was to promise that I would neither preach nor pray for any of the PRP men again.

After acquainting me with the *kaksuh,* Yun said I could go to sleep. It was 3:30 A.M. I crawled into an army cot next to the snoring Mr. Huh, pulled a khaki army blanket up over me, and did not sleep. At 7:00 A.M. we were up. The *kaksuh* had to be signed.

To have signed the first part would have been tacit admission that I accepted the KCIA charges that the eight men were Communists. I refused to sign, and much to my surprise, neither Huh nor Yun pushed me on it.

On the second part they did not give in so easily.

"You want me to say that I will obey all the policies of the government? Do you mean policies *(jongchaek)* or laws *(pub)?*"

"We mean policies. You are a foreigner here. You must obey all the policies."

"But there are too many policies, and some I do not agree with. How can you ask me to obey all policies? Not even you do that."

Huh was again "on his high horse." "Who do you think you are coming into our country and insulting our ways? You are a foreigner. Don't think that the American Embassy can help you. You can't break our laws!"

"I have lived in Korea for fifteen years and I've never been arrested or charged with breaking any laws. Nor do I intend to break any laws in the future. I willingly live under the laws of your land."

About this time a little man in army uniform came in and told Huh to hurry things up.

I got away with not having to sign part two of the *kuksuh*. On part three we comprised. They said they would take out the part about not praying for the men, and I said I would be willing to say that I would not talk about the PRP in my sermons.

At eleven o'clock or so the little army man took me to the office of deputy chief of security of the KCIA. The office was a large, plush, carpeted room. Mr. Lee, the man in charge, said he had lived in the United States for eight years and knew Americans very well. He was sorry to see me in this situation, but my offense, he said, had been very serious. "If you ever help the Communists again," he said, "I will either put you in prison or deport you." Then he ordered a black KCIA car to take me home.

Friends tell me that this particular Mr. Lee goes by many names. He was Mr. Kang when he lived in the United States as chief of the American section of the KCIA.

My arrest by the KCIA brought the case of the eight condemned men to the attention of many people who had previously not given it much thought. The paper I had written about these eight men and the so-called People's Revolutionary Party became widely distributed, and in prayer meetings and masses thousands of people began to hear the news that the "Communist conspiracy" announced in May of 1974 was in fact a lie, a fabrication of the KCIA itself. The eight men were in all probability innocent.

8

A VISIT BY THE PRESIDENT
OF THE UNITED STATES

On November 22, 1974, President Gerald Ford came to
Korea. That date had become a focal point of attention for
many people. Koreans have an incredibly optimistic view about
the United States. Despite everything, they still believe that
the U.S. government stands for democracy and freedom. They
are well aware that Park Chung Hee's biggest support has
come from America, but still there is the hope that the U.S. will
communicate to the Park regime that it will not continue to
support his dictatorial system. They know that they cannot
expect any help from Japan. Only the United States can possibly support them in their struggles to overcome the military
dictators. As the oppressions of Park Chung Hee and his KCIA
have increased, more and more often the question is asked,
"What's the difference between Park and Kim Il Song in the
North? They are both dictators." Park's tyranny inevitably
leads to a confusion as to what the difference between the
North and South really is. Such confusion is the exact environment that produces disintegration of society and invites Communist subversion.

Koreans do not want dictatorship by either the left or the
right. A middle ground of democracy and citizen participation
in government is a real option in Korea. The United States, the
Korean people hope, is surely interested in promoting this middle way. After all, is not the United States a great democracy?
Is it not in its interest to support democracy in other countries?

"When Ford comes, certainly he will do something to clarify the American position."

One group of women wrote directly to President Ford expressing their anxiety about his visit to their country.

Dear Mr. President:

God bless you and your family in this abundant season. We especially pray for your wife's complete recovery. We also pray for our friends, the American people, and for their limitless prosperity. We, who are addressing ourselves to you in this letter, are mothers of young people who have been sentenced to death, life imprisonment, and prison terms of 7, 10, 15 or 20 years for political reasons.

According to news reports, you will soon be visiting Korea. The people of Korea are pleased with your interest in our nation. However, the circumstances in which we now find ourselves, mean that there are some in Korea to whom your visit will bring sadness instead of happiness. In 1960, when former President Eisenhower visited our nation, we welcomed him with great excitement. Even today, the affection which we feel for you is no different from that time. However, circumstances today make it difficult to express the feelings which lie deep in our hearts. To speak frankly, we are frightened about the possible results of your visit. We are, in fact, so overcome with fear and concern, that we are sending this letter to you.

Our children, attempting to pattern their lives after Jesus Christ, have worked through student organizations to renew Korea. Because of this they are in prison convicted of being Communists and anti-government activists. They have all chosen to live and serve with the oppressed and rejected, the poor who labor in farms and rural areas. They have done this out of the deep conviction of their Christian faith. They have sought to assist the poor people in achieving a sense of pride and individual worth and to help them become independent members of society. Impressed by the lessons they have learned theoretically in school, they have worked to make democracy a reality.

Believing that God created man in his own image and that He wishes all to be free and blessed in His sight, our children have given of their sweat and tears to help free people from the injustices of our society. However, the Park regime, during its thirteen years in power, has demonstrated no real concern for the needs of the people, but has only been concerned for its own political survival. To this end it has enforced the so-called Yushin Constitution with the use of tanks and fabricated elections which have violated the rights of the people. Even one word spoken in opposition to this has branded the speaker as a communist.

Our children felt that they could not tolerate this situation and called upon the government to withdraw its Yushin Constitution. They were arrested and subjected to endless mental and physical tortures. Half-dead from the tortures, they were forced to sign confessions which have been used as evidence against them. Even now, behind prison bars and facing continued beatings and electric tortures, they are determined to continue their efforts to create a democratic Korea, believing that true freedom and peace for all are the will of God for society.

Therefore, we are concerned and deeply distressed by the possibility that President Park will use your visit to prolong his regime and lie to the people about the extent of your support for him. The prolongation of the Park regime can only mean continued unhappiness and despair for the people of Korea with no real security. We beg you to understand these feelings.

Because we mothers revealed what our sons actually said at their trials, we too have been arrested by the police and the Korean Central Intelligence Agency for severe interrogation. During the interrogations some of us were beaten to unconsciousness and had to be hospitalized for treatment. Even while undergoing treatment, agents of the KCIA came to interrogate us. They tormented us on our hospital beds and kept us from sleeping. A nurse who was helping to treat us broke down and wept at the treatment we were receiving.

Faced with the dread reality of the present, we mothers await your wise judgment and decision on our behalf. With a prayer for your peace and good health, we close our sad letter.

1974/10/20

Signed: (Representatives of mothers of prisoners)

Though not quite as optimistic as the Korean brethren, many of us American missionaries also had our attention focused on November 22. We knew that the American government already was well aware of what was going on in Korea, but we thought that a letter from us might help clarify some of the issues for President Ford. Sixty-two missionaries, Catholic, Presbyterian, Methodist, and Baptist, joined together in signing the letter. It read as follows:

Dear Mr. President:

The signers of this letter are all men and women who are living and serving in the Republic of Korea. Out of our deep concern for the welfare and development of Korea and its people, we wish to bring to your attention the critical situation now existing in this nation.

We are sure that you are aware of the imprisonment of scores of students, Christian clergymen, social leaders, lawyers and common citizens. These men and women have been arrested on false political charges. The military courts that have tried them have prostituted even military court standards, let alone standards of normal civil procedures. Sentences of several years to death have been handed down despite absence of evidence. Eight men are to die for their part in a so-called conspiracy which the government has not been able to prove ever existed.

In addition to these dramatic violations of human rights, countless citizens are under the ruthless surveillance of the Korean Central Intelligence Agency; professors at universities are examined lest they have "disloyal" ideas; businessmen are under constant police pressure to make political "contributions"; workers have had their rights to collective bargaining and collective action taken away; and ordinary citizens in the markets, tea rooms and other public places must carefully guard their speech lest they be overheard to offend the government in some manner.

These crimes against human rights and civil liberties are, however, only the by-product of a more fundamental problem; that being the "Yushin" Constitution ("Revitalizing Reforms"). This constitution, forcefully pressed upon the Korean people under a decree of martial law in October of 1972, eliminated democratic legislative government in Korea; made one man, Park Chung Hee, virtual dictator for life; and allowed Mr. Park and his CIA to suspend any person or group of their civil liberties at any time. The tragic events of 1974 are a consequence of this Yushin Constitution. Therefore large numbers of Korean people are demanding that the Yushin Constitution be withdrawn and the democratic constitution which existed up to 1972 be reinstated. This is a just demand which must be recognized if Korea is to return to the path of democracy and development.

Some rationalize that the Yushin Constitution and the suppression practiced by Park and his CIA are necessary in order to defend the country against a threatened invasion from North Korea. In fact, however, the observable results are the exact opposite. South Korea is so filled with mistrust and fear arising from Park's constitution and the resultant policies, that the social unity needed to defend against the North has certainly been weakened. Modernization of Korea's military cannot restore the confidence of the citizens in their government. Park's government has undermined its own military forces as well as those of the United States which just recently have again been pledged to defend the Republic of Korea.

How will the rest of the world react to America's continuing support of Park's dictatorial policies? The recent Congressional Hearings have clearly pointed out not only a shift in U.S. public opinion, but also the grave disadvantages of the U.S. continuing its unconditional support of the Park regime. We, too, are of the strong opinion that it would be in the best interest of both Korea and the U.S.—diplomatically, economically, and militarily—to convey strong disapproval of the trend of events in this country over the last few years. We feel that your visit, if it does not include this expression of disapproval, will only prove to millions of observers that the U.S. government does, in fact, fully support the oppressive policies of the present Korean government.

Mr. President, we are writing this letter out of love and commitment to the people of Korea. We wish you to be fully informed of these facts when you make your visit here in November. Already Korean newspapers have said that the government is likely to release some political prisoners before your visit. Of course, if this occurs, we, along with the people of Korea, will rejoice at such a move. However, at the same time we must recognize this act for what it is: only a gesture to impress the world and particularly the United States. We would mourn the fact that it was done with such motivation rather than as a genuine attempt to restore the integrity of this nation.

In light of these facts we ask that you strongly urge the leaders of the Republic of Korea to release *all* the political prisoners apprehended since October, 1972; to rescind the remaining Emergency Measures; and to abolish the Yushin Constitution, reinstating in its place the democratic constitution which existed up to October, 1972. We also strongly suggest that you meet with opposition religious, social, and political leaders.

We, the signers, representing various churches, agencies, and organizations, will be glad to meet with you or any of your accompanying party to discuss these matters directly. We pray that your visit will have some influence in healing the present tragic situation.

Sincerely yours,
The Undersigned

Two copies of the letter were sent to the White House. One was carried out of Korea by an American friend and posted in the U.S. The second one we decided to carry to the American ambassador in Korea and ask him to forward it to Mr. Ford. Five of us were entrusted with the task of getting the letter to the ambassador, Mr. Richard Sneider. It took three weeks before Ambassador Sneider would meet with us, but finally on Friday, October 25, word came from the embassy that we could meet with him on the following Monday. The format of the meeting, however, was to be changed. We had asked for a thirty to forty-five minute meeting so that the five of us could present the letter to President Ford and have a discussion with the ambassador. The ambassador, however, said that he would be willing to meet us, but at his house at the cocktail hour. He would also invite several other people to be present at the meeting. The embassy explained this change of plans by saying that Mr. Sneider was new at the job and he did not want the Korean government to get the impression that he had agreed to hold a meeting with "political activists." To protect himself from such misunderstanding, he decided to act as the host and invite "guests" to his house.

Some of us felt we should boycott the meeting. Our purpose was not to have a social gathering with some of the ambassador's invited guests. We represented 62 people, American citizens, who wanted to discuss serious issues with the ambassador of our government. Others advised attending. If we prepared well, it was argued, even the social hour planned by the ambassador could be used to accomplish our purposes. We would have to be sure to direct the discussion or it would certainly wander off into a hundred different topics.

A statement was prepared explaining the reasons why we had called the meeting and outlining some of the issues we wanted to bring before the ambassador and President Ford. With this statement in hand, we all agreed to go ahead with the meeting.

Thirteen guests and four embassy people were seated in a circle in the ambassador's residence. Ambassador Sneider said he was happy that we could all be there and hoped that in the months to come he would be able to get to know us on a first name basis. Today, he said, he would avoid the practice of making a long winded speech as ambassadors were sometimes prone to do. He wanted us to have a free and open discussion.

Father Jack Corcoran, head of the Maryknoll Order in Korea took the clue and spoke up. "Mr. Ambassador, as you know, five of us originally called this meeting. We represent sixty-two missionaries here in Korea, and before we get off on other things, we want to explain to you why we called the meeting. We've prepared a brief statement and George is going to read it for us."

The ambassador nodded his head and I began to read:

Mr. Ambassador, as you know, this meeting was requested by five of us who represent some sixty people who signed a letter addressed to President Ford. Most of the signers are men and women who have lived for a long number of years in Korea. Most of us are deeply involved in the lives of ordinary Korean people, and it is because of our deep involvement in their lives that we have felt compelled to address a letter to the President of the United States prior to his visit here in November.

We believe you have read the letter so we do not intend to read it again here, but we do want to explain to you and to President Ford the reasons why we have felt it necessary to express our deep concern over the present political situation in the Republic of Korea.

A. BACKGROUND

You are well acquainted with the events that have lead up to the present crisis, but let me trace just a few important dates.

1963. . .Establishment of a progressive-democratic constitution and initiation of the first five year economic plan. Free popular elections.

1967. . .Popular elections, and President Park Chung Hee was re-elected.
The second five year economic plan was begun. The first plan had been highly successful.

1969. . .President Park committed a coup against his own constitution so as to retain political power for an additional four years.

1971. . .In the absence of any crises, President Park declared a state of emergency and issued the so-called "National Protection Law" which put full control of Korean society into his hands.

1972. . .October . . . A declaration of marital law was declared, and under the suppression of martial law the Yushin Constitution was forced upon the nation.

1973. . .Easter . . . Rev. Pak Hyung Kyu and many others were arrested for distributing prayers for freedom and justice.
Autumn . . . Massive student demonstrations for freedom and democracy were held in all major universities over the country.

1974 . . .1/8 . . . In order to protect himself against mounting criticism, President Park announces the First Emergency Decree making it a crime to criticize the Yushin Constitution. A second decree established military courts to try offenders against the first decree.
1/17 . . . Eleven Christian pastors are arrested for issuing a statement criticizing the Yushin Constitution and asking for the re-instatement of democracy. Military courts subsequently sentenced these men to ten to fifteen years in prison.

The ambassador stood up, walked in front of my chair, picked up a dish of peanuts from a coffee table, passed it around and returned to his chair.

4/3 . . . A wave of abortive demonstrations were held by university students. President Park issued the fourth emergency decree making it an offense punishable by death to demonstrate against the government. The decree is applied retroactively to university students who took part in the demonstrations of that day.

4/25 . . . The Korean CIA declares it has broken a huge Communist conspiracy aimed at the bloody overthrow of the government and the establishment of a peasant-proletariat Communist government.

Over 1200 people were arrested and about 200 were given sentences by military courts of from ten years to death. These extreme sentences have been given by military courts held in virtual secrecy. Little or no evidence has been produced by the government to support its claim that there was a Communist conspiracy. Indeed every indication is that the so-called "conspiracy" was a fabrication of the KCIA used to strengthen its hand against all critics of the government. The Communist conspiracy charge attempts to play on the real fears of the people in order to maintain President Park's political control of the nation.

Since President Park's coup against his own constitution in 1969, he and his government have followed a consistent path toward dictatorship. The people have tried to resist and preserve what they had of democracy, but their protests have only brought increased suppressions.

B. COMMUNISM

Some claim that the present totalitarianism is required by the threat of North Korean Communism. While the threat from the North cannot be minimized, it must be remembered that the peak of that threat would appear to have been around 1968. Yet no state of emergency was then declared. Nor were basic liberties repealed. Despite constant government assertions to the contrary the threat from the North has certainly declined since then, and cannot be accepted as a justification for an oppressive system set up in 1972.

C. ECONOMIC DEVELOPMENT

The government also claims that its current practices are necessary in order to safeguard its program of economic development, but here too the argument is spurious. Korea's great economic development began in 1963 and moved through two very successful five year plans *before* any of the so-called Yu-shin system was established. There can be no claim that Park's Yushin system, initiated in 1972, has any causal relationship with Korea's impressive economic development.

Again I became aware that Mr. Sneider's seat was empty. This time he was pouring coffee. As I continued to read, it occurred to me that perhaps the ambassador was demonstrating technique for the benefit of the two Korean waiters who were standing stiffly nearby.

D. MILITARY STABILITY

It is also claimed that dictatorial control is required in order to provide for basic military stability vis á vis the North, but as our letter explains, military stability rests upon social unity. The present regime has made a shambles of social unity in South Korea and has to that extent undermined its own military as well as the military forces of the U.S. committed to this country.

E. U.S.A. INFLUENCE

1. The above facts have been communicated by us to many American congressmen and senators, both through writing and direct conversation. Now that President Ford is coming to Korea we want to express these same concerns to him.

2. Ever since the end of the Second World War, the U.S.A. has exercised a strong influence on Korean development. These influences have been in the military, economic, social, international and political sectors. The U.S.A. has worked along with the people of the Republic of Korea in almost every facet of domestic and foreign affairs, and much of that influence has been for the building up of democracy and human dignity.

3. Now, however, we see the U.S.A. drawing back from its commitment to democracy. Once again, as it has done so often in South America, Chile and Vietnam, the U.S.A. appears to be accepting the fallacy that the delusory stability of a dictator is more in the self-interest of the U.S.A. than is the development of a free democratic society.

4. Despite the establishment of an oppressive dictatorship by Park Chung Hee our U.S.A. government has at every turn acted faithfully to support him.

   a. Secretary Kissinger is reported to have stated that the
      U.S. support here has nothing to do with internal affairs.
   b. Secretary of Agriculture Butz made a visit and promised
      increased help through the 480 program.
   c. David Kennedy leads a group of U.S.A. investors to
      Korea.
   d. Military support for Korea is continued at previous lev-
      els despite strong House opposition.
   e. Mr. Dorsey of Gulf Oil brings another group of American
      investors to Korea. Dow Chemicals plans $200 million in
      investment.
   f. President Gerald Ford visits Korea.

For a third time Sneider stood up. This time it was the
dried fish that needed passing. I stopped reading and watched
him. He looked around at me, gave the fish to someone else and
returned to his chair. He very courteously then remained
seated throughout the rest of my reading.

   5. All of this has taken place in the same year that the Korean
      people have protested the loudest against their government
      and in the year when the Park government has most vio-
      lently suppressed its own people. The conclusions that can-
      not be avoided are:
      a. The U.S.A. cares little for democracy in Korea;
      b. The U.S.A. is primarily concerned with the expansion of
         its own economic capitalism into Korea;
      c. The U.S.A. accepts military dictatorship as the funda-
         mental defender of U.S.A. interests in Korea.
   6. We as Americans do not want to accept such conclusions.
      We feel there is still a chance for our government to act on
      behalf of democracy in Korea. We are not asking the U.S.
      government or the U.S. CIA to overthrow the Park govern-
      ment, but we are asking, as stated in our letter, that Presi-
      dent Ford clearly communicate to President Park a request
      that:
      a. All political prisoners sentenced since October of 1972
         be released; and
      b. That the Yushin Constitution be abolished and the old
         constitution be restored. We also ask that President

Ford communicate with opposition political and social leaders.

In this manner the U.S.A. can let it be known that it has not forgotten its own commitment to freedom.

Mr. Ambassador, we ask you to forward this letter to President Ford, and we ask you to communicate to him our concern as expressed in this statement. We also request an opportunity to meet with some representative of President Ford's party when it comes in November.

Thank you.

"Does anyone else have anything to say?" the ambassador asked as soon as I had finished reading.

Sister Jean Malone, of the Maryknoll Order, a nurse who for long years had served Korea's rural and urban poor people, spoke up. "I just want to report that recently there are a lot of people asking the question, 'What is the difference between the government we have here and the kind they have in the North?' People are afraid the dictatorship here is getting as bad as it is under Communism."

This must have been the cue that the ambassador was waiting for. For the next half hour he lectured us on the superiority of societies like South Korea over the Communist systems of North Korea and Eastern Europe. Curiously, he ended his lecture with Chile. "Some people accuse us of interfering in the internal affairs of Chile, but that is nonsense . . . well, perhaps we did contribute six million dollars, but everyone knows you can't create a revolution with only six million dollars."

Our meeting with Mr. Sneider was far from a success. It left a bad taste in everyone's mouth. We had hoped for serious dialogue and we got a half-baked lecture. Nevertheless, the ambassador did promise he would forward our letter on to President Ford. I wonder if it ever got there? We never received any acknowledgement whatsoever.

As the day for Ford's visit came closer, the KCIA tightened its surveillance. Universities were all closed down. Extra troops of agents and riot police were dispatched to the Protestant prayer meetings and the Catholic masses. No incidents of protest were to be allowed to mar the show that Park's government had planned for Mr. Ford.

But the authorities underestimated the power of angry women. The day before Ford arrived a group of thirty women whose husbands, sons, or daughters were in prison for political reasons, arrived a few at a time in front of the American Embassy. Suddenly they unrolled signs and donned head bands and dashed into the embassy compound. They sat down inside the fence blocking incoming traffic. The signs called for the restoration of democracy and the head bands for the release of their loved ones.

The demonstration lasted for only a few brief minutes. Riot police in full battle gear arrived on the scene, marched into the embassy compound, picked up the women and threw them onto the bus. Father Jim Sinnott, when he saw how the police were treating the women, lost his temper and charged into the police flicking their gladiator-like helmets down over their eyes. Needless to say, he was grabbed by several of the police and carted off along with the women. Some months after that Father Sinnott was forced to leave Korea. The Park government said he had participated in political action. In fact his "crime" was that he could not contain himself in face of cruelty and injustice.

Ford arrived at 9:00 A.M., November 22. The streets were lined with people. Probably no one told the American President that the children waving their flags had all been assigned by the authorities to occupy certain locations, and that the large number of men standing along the route was in fact the national guard in civilian clothes. The national guard all over Seoul was ordered to be along the parade route to make sure the crowds would be both large and orderly.

Ford's visit was a victory for Park and a defeat for the democratic forces of Korea. Apparently, "national security" and military defense dominated the talks between the two governments. Nothing was reported that would indicate that Ford had anything to say to the Park regime about its dictatorial oppressions. The people's hope in the United States had once more been in vain.

At our meeting with Ambassador Sneider we had asked that someone from Ford's party talk with us and with various leaders of Korean society, but we had been given no reply. During the afternoon of November 22, President Ford's Press Secretary Ron Nessen was asked by a newspaper reporter whether there would be a meeting with missionaries. Nessen replied that he would get back to that matter later on. We waited, but there was no word. Finally, at 9:30 P.M., we decided that the Ford visit must not be let pass without some communication being made on behalf of the people and the political prisoners. Since President Ford had given no indication that he wanted to hear from us, we decided to make known our message to the public. We called a press conference. At 9:30 P.M. reporters from the *New York Times,* the *Washington Post,* the *Los Angeles Times,* the NBC News, CBS News, and a few free lance writers met with us at the President Hotel. The conference covered the background of our letter to President Ford, our meeting with Ambassador Sneider, and the issues of political dictatorship and KCIA operations.

When I arrived back home at 11:30 P.M., Dorothy informed me that there had been a phone call from the American Embassy. Mr. Richard Smyser, a member of the presidential party, wanted to meet with us at 10:00 A.M. the next morning. The call from the embassy had come at 10:30 P.M., one hour after our news conference had begun. Would Mr. Smyser have wanted to see us if there had been no press conference? I think probably not. More than ample time had been available for such a meeting to have been scheduled, yet it was not. And then suddenly at 10:30 at night we were told that Smyser would deliberately stay over in Korea for a few hours, after Ford left, so that he could talk with us. If there had been no press conference, Smyser would probably have taken off at 8:00 A.M. along with his boss.

The discussion with Mr. Smyser, who was introduced to us as the senior member of the National Security Council, was something less than a discussion. He refused to comment on anything. His function, he told us, was to report all that we had to say back to the White House. He was not authorized to talk or discuss. So for an hour and a half Smyser laboriously wrote down every word that we said. Whether he indeed took our words to the White House and Mr. Ford we shall never know. Since then we have heard nothing from Smyser or the White House. Subsequent statements by the American government about the Korean situation completely ignore the issues which we raised. Smyser's sacrifice of a few hours to talk with the missionaries looks like a sop to appease us and subvert any effect that our news conference might have had.

Modernization of the Korean military and the expansion of American capital into Korean business are the categories that impress men like Smyser and the American government. Human rights, justice, and democracy are pie-in-the-sky niceties that Christians talk about. The *New Yorker* magazine stated the American government's attitude toward Korea in one precise sentence: "The plain fact is that for some years now the American government has regarded ruthless, dictatorial regimes as safe havens for American interests." We missionaries had hoped to "influence" our government away from such madness, but our hopes, like those of the Korean people, were in vain. There was no way the State Department was going to pay heed to anything we said.

Our meeting with Smyser took place in the American embassy. As we prepared to leave, we noticed that standing just outside the embassy compound was a battery of newsmen— Korean, American, and Japanese. They were waiting for us and would expect a statement. We agreed on a short statement that said something to the effect that we had attempted to communicate to Mr. Smyser some of the problems of human rights as they have been expressed by Korean church leaders in the last year. I was delegated to give this statement to the reporters.

Despite the innocuousness of the statement, our meeting with Smyser was given big play by the Korean newspapers. What we represented contrasted sharply with what Ford and

Kissinger had done during their day's visit to Korea. The thing that made the Smyser meeting important to Korea, however, was that an official representative of the President of the United States had been told the truth about Korea's military dictatorship.

We hoped that our communication to this official representative of the American President would do some good. The Korean government apparently was afraid it would do some good, for one of the reasons that I was expelled from Korea, only three weeks after Ford's visit, was that I had acted as spokesman for the group of missionaries that met with Smyser.

9

LAST WEEK

On December 5th a phone call came from the embassy. The deputy ambassador, Richard Erickson, wanted to see me for lunch the next day. It was, he said, urgent.

At 12:00 noon I went to the embassy. Mr. Erickson and Mr. Cleveland met me. The three of us then were driven over to Erickson's private residence for lunch. After the usual awkward niceties we got down to business.

Mr. Lho Shin Yong, Assistant Foreign Minister for the Republic of Korea, had visited Mr. Erickson and told him that the Korean government had decided to deport me. The charges against me, he said, were two: on October 10th I had preached a sermon praising the Communists; and in a sermon at Huksuk Dong Methodist Church on November 24th, I had criticized the *Yushin* system of government.

The first sermon, of course, was the one for which I had been interrogated on October 11th. The second sermon was the one I had preached on behalf of Methodist clergymen sentenced to long years in prison by kangaroo military courts. I had traced the ministry of Rev. Kim Kyung Nak as he served factory workers in the name of Christ. I told of how the KCIA interfered in the lives of the workers and how local union leaders had been threatened and beaten. And I related how Reverend Kim, along with other clergymen, had come under attack by the KCIA because they had dared stand for the rights of the workers. It was the tyranny of the KCIA that finally motivated the clergy to protest against the Park government.

So, in fact, I had criticized Park's government. I had criticized its use of the KCIA to further humiliate the nation's poor and I had criticized its persecution of Christian clergymen who spoke for justice. I was guilty of what Mr. Lho charged. But at the time I spoke, it was not illegal to criticize the government. The decree forbidding criticism had been temporarily rescinded. And, of course, Mr. Lho had made no mention of the fact that his information about the content of my sermons had come from the KCIA agents who attend church services and record everything that is preached and prayed. In today's Korea it is the KCIA which determines what is acceptable for Christians to say or do.

Unless I apologized for these two sermons, Lho said, I would be deported. I had until the afternoon of Monday, December 9th, to send my apology to the government.

Erickson communicated Lho's message to me in a straightforward way without giving advice or suggestion. In the context of the time I was not surprised that Korea's KCIA would move against me or anyone else who would question its right to rule. But I was completely unprepared for the manner in which the attack against me came. A visit by a couple of friendly agents, as in October, would not have been unexpected, but to be sitting in the plush dining room of the Deputy Ambassador of the United States and have him tell me in a calm, matter-of-fact voice that I was going to be kicked out of Korea was a bit unsettling. "I wish," I said, "there was some way of avoiding this coup. This is my home, where my children were born. But I cannot answer now. The problem is not my private one. It involves my Korean and missionary brethren. I will have to talk with them first."

The next morning another call came from Erickson. Lho had again visited the embassy and was extremely angry when he heard my reply. Lho, it seems, thought the American embassy should have forced me to write an apology on the spot. The threat of expulsion was repeated. Erickson said that he had told Lho that he would no longer act as middleman. Lho

would have to deal with me directly. That was the last I heard
from Erickson.

Immediately after leaving Erickson's house on the 6th, I
began to consult with my missionary and Korean colleagues. In
each instance I was advised to stand firm. "Do not apologize!"
Very few of them thought the government would actually go so
far as to carry out the threat. I hoped against hope that they
were right, but I felt Lho had so committed himself that neither
he nor the government could back off.

Late Sunday night word came from Ed Poitras, a Methodist missionary, that I should walk down over the hill to talk
with a friend of ours. In order to maintain the anonymity of this
friend we shall call him Mr. Shin. Shin is a personal friend of
both the Lho Shin Yongs and the Kim Chong Pils. Kim is prime
minister of Korea. Shin had visited the prime minister's house
seeking some way by which a compromise could be worked out,
but he was adamant; "Ogle must apologize, and then we can
talk. There is no other way."

Mr. Shin had also called Lho Shin Yong, asking him to at
least meet with me and hear what I had to say. Lho likewise
refused to meet me. I have been told since then that the decision to expel me had come from Park Chung Hee himself. If so,
that would explain why both Kim and Lho refused to talk to
me. When a general gives a command, the underlings carry it
out. They do not discuss it.

I left Shin's house that night knowing full well there was
no out. It was a simple matter of apologize or be forced to leave.
I did not want to leave. I had always found life in Korea to be
stimulating and satisfying. There were many of the brothers
and sisters to whom I could be of assistance, especially the
wives and families of those in prison. I wanted to continue
working with Rev. Cho Wha Soon, Cho Sung Hyuk, Yu Hong
Shik and others. And there was my own family. I knew none
of them wanted to leave. Martin was in the middle of basketball
season. Kathy was deeply involved in a small fellowship of
young Christian girls. Karen and Kristy were enjoying their
school life, and my wife had just begun a nursing job which she

seemed to be enjoying. "Maybe I should just write some kind of an innocuous statement of regret without actually apologizing. Maybe that would be enough. How could I word it?"

On the other hand, however, to write any kind of a letter of regret or apology would have some predictable consequences. First, it would mean that I was breaking communion with the many brothers and sisters who had willingly accepted long prison terms rather than write such apologies. Second, it would be tantamount to a denial of most of my ministry in Korea. The people on whose behalf I had spoken in my sermons were indeed the oppressed and imprisoned, the least of Christ's brethren. To say that I regretted speaking out for them would have contradicted my entire ministry among the factory workers and poor of Korea.

And, thirdly, any form of apology would be used against me by the KCIA. The KCIA is not an ordinary police force. It is a military secret police that has the one objective of crushing everyone it thinks is an enemy of the Park regime. A letter of apology in their hands would have been used to blackmail or threaten me for the rest of my life.

I walked along up the hill that Sunday night, December 8, 1974, with the pros and cons waging a war inside my brain. But then suddenly the war was settled. It was resolved inside me, almost as though the computer had acquainted itself with all the data and reached a decision. It was formulated in my brain in one short Korean sentence: *kojin mal haji marla* (Do not lie). I finished my walk home knowing what I had to do.

Lho Shin Yong had demanded that a letter of apology reach him by the afternoon of the next day. After arriving home I sat down at the table and wrote him a letter.

Dear Mr. Lho:

I have been informed by the American Embassy in Seoul that the government of the Republic of Korea has decided to deport me. I have lived in Korea as a Methodist missionary for almost fifteen years, and in all that time I have considered myself to be under the laws of the Korean government. Therefore, I find it difficult to understand why at this time, on such a serious matter, the government has not communicated to me directly.

I am to be deported from the country I love without any clear statement of charges against me. Verbal, second-handed information given through the American Embassy has been the only means used to communicate to me. If I have acted in a manner that requires my deportation, should I not at least be given an official and written statement of charges against me?

I love Korea and wish to live here for many years to come, so I ask that you give to me in writing a statement of charges so that I can make a defense.

I have also been informed by the American Embassy that you wish to have a written statement of my intentions. Therefore, I am enclosing such a statement with this letter.

Sincerely yours,
Rev. George Ogle

The statement I wrote was very brief, and I am sure it was not the type of statement Mr. Lho was looking for.

Statement of Intention

Jesus Christ was a poor man. He lived and died for the salvation of Man's soul and society. I have intended that my acts as a missionary in Korea should follow that path. I have no political or social ambitions and support no political party. I do, however, intend to preach Christ's message of salvation, freedom and justice, and to serve those who are suffering.

The next morning a missionary friend carried my letter and statement to Minister Lho's office. Lho, however, made no response. I never heard another word from him, nor has any government official ever presented an official set of charges against me.

It was not until the afternoon of the next day that the government took action. I was at home preparing a lecture for one of my university classes when our cook came and told me two KCIA agents had come for me. I told her to tell them I was not home, but would be back in an hour or so. Then I made a phone call. Some of us missionaries had agreed on a system whereby if any of us were threatened with arrest we would quickly notify everyone else. I made one call, and waited. I was alone. Dorothy and the kids were at school. I had no way of knowing when or whether I would see them again, but I wanted to share with them the emotion of those moments. I wrote them a message:

> The KCIA is outside. I'm scared. Strange! I'm sure they won't beat or torture me, but the thought of being under the complete power of men like that puts fear and humiliation in my heart.
>
> I pray. Christ is very real, but the burden that evil is about and holds the ace card is not removed. I've tried to be honest with myself and others. I am not a reformer, nor a radical. But I find no sense to life other than the freedom and faith I find in Christ. The love of these is all I have to pass on to my children whom I love more than life.
>
> I pray for Kim Kyung Nak, Pak Hyung Kyu, Kim Chan Kook, Lee Hai Hak and all the others. Mine is nothing compared to theirs, but I hope I am of one mind and one heart. I pray for their speedy release. I pray for the speedy death of the evil which has caused such senseless suffering. The military men who think of their own people as enemies and each problem as a military objective to over run are ruining the progress, the beauty of Korea. May God forgive them.
>
> I remember the fifteen years of joy that I've had in Korea. I thank God. I thank Him for Cho Sung Hyuk and his beautiful wife, Cho Wha Soon, Yu Hong Shik, Choe Yung Hei, Miss Yu, Miss Kwak of Inchun. How can I ever thank them?
>
> I remember the small house we lived in in Inchun. Our children were born there. The warm ondal floor, the love. Our neighbor who spoke the southern dialect of Andong and drove me up the wall.
>
> The hours spent walking around Inchun's factories. I remember Choe Myung In, Chang Tong Hi and so many of the workers and Christian laymen dedicated to decency and justice.
>
> Now! Guess it's time to go. God be praised.

Friends had begun to arrive. Within a few minutes fifteen to twenty people were gathered in the house. Dorothy and the kids arrived. Friends cannot protect you from the devil, but they can give you courage. Finally several of us walked outside to where the KCIA men were patiently waiting. Only then did we learn that these particular men had not come from the

KCIA. They were agents from the immigration office. I told them I was ready to go. They chided me for making them wait so long. Permission was given for one other person to ride along with me, and off we went to the immigration office. This was the first of three such rides I would take before the week was over.

When we got to the immigration office, my friend was refused entry and I alone was ushered into the office of the director of immigration.

Interrogation by the immigration people is little different from that practiced by the KCIA over at South Mountain. In my case the major difference was that at South Mountain I was required to write down (in Korean, of course) both the questions that the interrogator asked and the answers that I gave. At the immigration they had a man who did all the recording for us. Otherwise the purpose and method were exactly the same. The purpose is to get the one being interrogated to confess to the crime that the interrogator says he committed. The method is an endless series of devious questions interspersed with harangues by the interrogator. You are told that you have broken the Korean laws, that you have contempt for Korean customs, that you lack sincerity, and that you are arrogant.

I was asked about my background, about people I knew, my work with UIM, and my sermon of October 10th where I spoke about the eight men condemned to death. There were, however, two new items of importance. The first related to my position as lecturer at Seoul National University. I had been invited by the dean of the College of Commerce to teach at Seoul National. The school authorities knew my background and they knew that I was a Methodist missionary. I entered Korea September 29, 1973 on a missionary visa, and proceeded to teach as I had contracted to do.

Now, a year later, immigration officials all of a sudden claimed that my missionary visa did not permit me to teach in a university. I had broken Korean law, the interrogator said, by teaching at Seoul National University. He demanded that I confess to having trespassed against the law and to having violated my visa.

This was the only thing they could manufacture about my

having broken the law. Yet the interrogator over and over again disdainfully referred to me as a lawbreaker.

(About a month later the Prime Minister of Korea, Kim Chong Pil, during a public speech, called me a liar. He said I had confessed to breaking the law while I was at the immigration office and yet had denied doing so when I spoke to other people. Kim, of course, did not venture to say which law it was that I had supposedly confessed to having broken, but apparently he was borrowing the interrogator's approach that I had violated my visa by teaching at the university. Strange, however, that the prime minister of a nation in a public speech would feel called upon to defend his government's actions by the rather crass manner of calling me a liar.)

The other unique part of the interrogation by the immigration people was that my interrogator raised basic theological issues. One series of questions and answers went like this:

Question: No man can perfectly know the will of God. Is that not correct?

(*Reflection before answering:* What is this? Where is he going? To say that we can perfectly know His will is foolish. To say that we can't will allow him to say, "Then how do you know what you are doing is the will of God? It is a question about authority. Since you can't know God's perfect will, you as an individual must obey the state.")

Answer: Are you a theologian? If not, you have no qualification to make such a statement. Knowledge of God's will is one of theology's most profound subjects.

Question: Christians believe in the Bible don't they? Yet everyone interprets the Bible for himself. Each person has to interpret it in his own way. Isn't that true?

(*Reflection before answering:* What is the aim of this one? It's the same question. If I agree, he says, "See this is all your own individual hangup. You're only one person and the government speaks for the whole nation.")

Answer: Christians are not left as isolated individuals to interpret Scripture according to their whims. There is always a church, or denomination, a community or a group that interprets and applies the Bible. I can introduce you to thousands of Korean Christians who interpret the Bible just as I do.

Question: Are Christians, then, not required to obey the law? You can go breaking the law anytime you want. You have to obey the government don't you?

Answer: Probably more than other people Christians are law abiding citizens. I have lived in Korea for fifteen years, but have not broken the laws. I respect Korean law and customs, but in those matters where there is a conflict between the teachings of Scripture and the orders of a government, then I obey my faith.

On the first day the questioning went on for five hours. Two days later, December 12th, I was again under interrogation. It was much a repeat of the first day. At the end of the second day, about 9:30 at night, however, an event occurred for which I shall always be thankful.

The interrogator was once again trying to get me to "reflect" upon my wrongdoings and write a statement of regret concerning the problems "I had caused." In the midst of his exhortations for sincere reflection he began to yell, "Do you think having people demonstrate for you is going to help you? You have got to be sincere. People praying and singing and demonstrating won't be of any use to you!"

His words to me were like a cup of cool water. The interrogation had gone on for seven or more hours. I had a headache that felt like some little man was beating drums inside my head. I was bushed. I had had no idea that anyone was praying or demonstrating for me. The news did not relieve my headache, but it allowed me to relax. I was not fighting the battle alone.

"Do you think such things will save you?" shouted the interrogator.

"No, I guess not, but if there are any brothers and sisters praying and demonstrating for me, I can only thank God."

I had no way of knowing what was going on, of course, but what had made the interrogator so angry was this: a group of about seventy-five friends had gathered in a room at the Na-

tional Council of Churches' Building and had declared that
they would remain there singing and praying until I was
released; at the same time there was a mass being said at the
Myung Dong Catholic Cathedral. At times during the mass
word was announced about my being under interrogation and
prayers were offered in my behalf. Also, a group of about two
dozen missionary friends had kept a silent vigil standing for
some seven to eight hours outside the immigration office. Such
community of spirit has become a common experience for
many of Korea's Christians. It was an experience that I was to
enjoy several times in the next few days. When I was finally
released that night (December 10th), the officials would not
allow me to join the friends waiting for me, for along with them
there was a small battery of newspaper reporters. The courage
and commitment of some of Korea's press have supplied new
hoeroes in the battle for a free press. The men of the *Tonga Ilbo*
newspaper were especially courageous and personally helpful
to me. The KCIA and the immigration authorities were outraged by this newspaper. They were afraid of the effect on the
people if the truth were published. (That is why they finally
used "goons" at 3:30 A.M. on the morning of March 17, 1975, to
occupy the newspaper offices and throw out the writers and
reporters. Since then the *Tonga Ilbo* has been in captivity to
the KCIA.)

On the night of December 10th the immigration authorities escorted me directly home rather than allow me to talk
with friends and reporters.

The next day I tried to rest. I unplugged our telephone and
lay down. Before long the doorbell rang. It was the telephone
company man. He had come to fix our phone. I explained that
someone was sick in the house and needed to rest. I had unplugged the phone.

"But you can't do that! This phone is the company's and
has to be kept plugged in all the time. You have caused us a lot
of trouble. Your phone has been ringing all morning!" retorted
the man. He pushed his way into the room to reattach the
phone.

"What do you mean I can't do that? I bought the phone. If I don't want to answer it that's my privilege. Get out!"

An argument of shouting and threats followed. I am sure the fellow was only doing his job, but at that particular moment, I could have throttled him. Now I wish I could apologize to him for having treated him as I did.

Just after the telephone man left, a message came informing me that the General Conference of our Korean Methodist Church, which had been in session since December 9th, wanted me to appear before it that evening to tell the delegates my side of the deportation problem.

When I arrived at the conference, I was met by the bishop. His words to me were, "When you speak, keep it short. Don't say anything about the political prisoners or the government. Just tell them you are sorry that so much commotion has developed."

I could not believe my ears. I thought I had been asked to speak my side of the story. "Bishop, if that is what you want, why did you ask me to come? I cannot do that."

I put my coat back on and started to walk out. As I turned away, one of the older pastors, a friend for many years, took my arm. We walked to the back of the church together.

"Wait," he said, "until the end of the opening worship service. There will be a call for you from the floor."

I waited.

As soon as the closing prayer was over, five or six of the delegates stood up demanding that I be given time to speak. The pastor who had advised me to stay led me up to the podium. We were met with a standing, prolonged ovation. Never have I ever received such a welcome. These were men and women, friends, among whom I had lived for fifteen years. They were applauding not just to support me, but to show their solidarity with the witness that their fellow Christians were giving all over the country.

I tried to talk but could not. I cried. The emotion of that communion was too much. Others were also crying. It took a couple of minutes before I could begin to talk. I briefly reviewed the cases of Rev. Kim Kyung Nak and Rev. Cho Wha Soon as examples of the unjust sufferings that Christians were undergoing because of the KCIA. I told them how I had asked Christians to pray for the eight men condemned by the military courts. I could not write the apology that the government demanded, I said, because to do so would be a repudiation of my entire ministry and a betrayal of my brothers and sisters in prison. Finally I assured them that neither Kim Kyung Nak, Cho Wha Soon, nor I had acted in any way because of political motivation or political purposes. We were attempting to be faithful to the gospel of Jesus. That is why they were in prison and I was to be deported. I read Luke 4:18, asked for their prayers, and walked down from the pulpit.

Again the General Conference delegates arose and expressed themselves through a long and loud ovation. The Conference then adopted a statement strongly criticizing unjust government practices and demanding that the threat of deportation against me be withdrawn. At the motion of one of Methodism's most well known revival preachers, two men were delegated the responsibility of carrying the statement directly to the government by 10:00 A.M. the next morning.

By 7:00 A.M. the next morning, however, the immigration men were again at my front gate. This time I was told to bring my passport. At the immigration office the interrogator, the head of the immigration office, and the recorder and I again faced each other, and the interrogator began once more to take us on a repeat of all that we had gone over on the two previous days. After an hour or so, I had had it.

"If you have new questions to ask, I will try to answer, but if you insist on going back over everything again, I will not say another word unless you supply me with an interpreter who is completely fluent in English."

"You refuse to answer questions?"

"I have nothing more to say about the matters we have already covered."

The interrogator and chief of immigration got up and went out of the room. In a short while the chief returned. He sat behind his big desk and told me to stand in front of it. Then he handed me a paper that said I was to be deported. At first he said I would be kept in jail until the time of deportation, but a little while later after he had again left the office and come back in, he said that I would be kept under house arrest.

I asked him if he had made the decision to deport me on the basis of our talks over the last week. He refused an answer.

"I know that you had no part in the decision. Who was it, Kim Chong Pil?"

At the mention of this name, the chief became very agitated and told me to sit down and shut up.

The interrogations at the immigration office were, of course, a pure hoax. The decision had already been made, as Lho Shin Yong told the American Embassy on December 5th. Certain formalities must be kept up in order to deceive the public. My interrogations at the immigration office were just that, a deception. If I had signed their apology sometime during the interrogation, all the better for them, but in any case the Korean government could always say that I had been given a hearing according to law.

News travels fast. By the time the authorities got me back home, the house was jammed with police, KCIA agents, newsmen, and friends. First came the interview with the press. The police kept trying to get them out of the house. I insisted they were my guests in my house and had a right to stay. Dorothy and I sat on the couch and talked with them for perhaps an hour before they left. A couple of them whom I knew personally said they would stay around outside in case I needed them.

As the newsmen thinned out, so did the KCIA and police. One policeman in uniform drew me aside and said he had been ordered to guard our house so that no one could get in. I asked if he would keep his men outside. He said he would do so, and if I had any need I should let him know. He was older than the rest of the crowd that occupied our house just then. His eyes and tone of voice suggested a sadness about the duty he had to perform.

Gradually the house emptied. About a dozen friends were

left. We talked and cried, prayed and sang, and in the midst of our sorrow in walked Ruth Burkholder carrying a beautiful, big angel food cake with peppermint icing. The house by that time was surrounded not only by the regular police, but by two or three busloads of riot police in full battle gear. Others had been turned back, but Ruth somehow walked in among them and delivered the cake undamaged. Dorothy made coffee and we ate the angel food cake in a communion that was of the spirit of the last supper.

Around three o'clock a man from the American Embassy arrived. He brought with him a list of Korean lawyers I could call. It was much too late for that, but we did try two men, one of whom was away and one of whom refused to become involved. The embassy man also told us that they had been told unofficially that I was going to be taken at five o'clock.

A radio news broadcast at about the same time reported a release from the Ministry of Justice which said I was being deported for "public demonstrations and mass agitation of the people." Details as to what demonstrations, what agitations they were talking about were, of course, omitted. The news broadcast also said I would be leaving that same day.

At five o'clock a man from immigration came to the door and announced that I would have to be ready to go in thirty minutes. Dorothy had already packed my bag. She and the children would stay. There was no way we could have closed the house and all left together. I had little fear that they would be in danger. The KCIA would have had nothing to gain from harming them.

Dorothy, Martin, Kathy, Karen, Kristy and I went upstairs to be alone. We sang a hymn, "Jesus Is All the World to Me," had a prayer and said good-bye. Downstairs there was Gene Matthews, Sister Dolores, Olin Burkholder, Sue and Randy Rice, Sister Madge, Father Price, Coffee Worth, and Sister Sigrid. We prayed and blessed each other and parted. Martin took my bag and carried it out to the black car waiting for me. In that moment I felt a great surge of pride in our children. They had gone through a considerable hell in the last few days, but they had done more than held their own. Martin, 14, carried my bag out in the midst of police and crying people with an apparent calmness that gave me courage.

Looking back on the incident Kathy, 13, wrote, "I support Daddy wholly on all of his actions and it hurts bitterly when people don't understand . . . but I know that what I feel is only a fraction of what Dad feels." Her support came through to me loud and clear, as did Karen's, who was 10. Karen wrote these words: "Really in my heart I was very, very proud to be an Ogle, but some days I didn't want to go to school for some of my classmates didn't understand and would ask nerve-wracking questions."

I thought a prayer of thanks for the kids and Dorothy as I walked out the door toward the car. Before I got to the car, however, someone, an English-speaking person whom I can't remember, pressed into my hand a small gold ring. "This is (a personal ring) from one of the ladies." I slipped it onto my little finger and again cried. I knew instinctively it was from Mrs. Woo Hong Sun whose husband was condemned to die. She is the woman who had confessed that she and her husband had fallen in love when they were young, twenty years ago, and still, at the ages of 42, held hands. She had been standing outside our yard all that afternoon. When she saw me being taken away, she was afraid that I would end up in Japan or the United States without money or anywhere to go, so she quickly took her own gold ring and threw it to the friend who then gave it to me.

I wrote to Mrs. Woo a few days later that I would wear the ring until her husband was free and then I would bring it back to her. This promise I will never be able to keep. Park Chung Hee had her husband hanged on April 9, 1975. They had never had a chance to see each other after his arrest a year earlier.

I sat in the middle between two men in the back seat. Two others occupied the front seat. As the car pulled away I became aware for the first time that the riot police were being confronted by 75 to 100 shouting and chanting people. The road was blocked, but an advance by the club-wielding riot police quickly opened it up. The car moved slowly down the hill. Over the heads of the riot cops I caught a glimpse of our church pastor shouting in anger. There was Mrs. Woo. There was Father Daley. Cho Wha Soon, Mr. Whang. Faces escaped me as the car speeded up, but just as we were about past the crowd a woman wearing a white hat broke away from the police and ran down the hill beside the car beating it with her fists, shouting, "Come back, come back!" Then she, too, was gone and I was alone except for the four black-suited men seated around me. It was dark.

We did not go through the airport terminal. The gates leading directly onto the landing field clattered open as we approached. Our car did not even slow down. We went straight through and immediately the gates swung shut behind us. The car moved up beside a building and stopped. I was told to get out. I and my suitcase were transferred to a Volkswagen van type of vehicle. Inside the van there were about ten men. Under their guard, I was then driven up to the entrance of a large 747 airliner, Korean Airlines, flight 002. Before I got out I turned to the men in the van and said, "I have lived in your country for fifteen years. I thank you for that. Since I am not allowed to say goodbye to my friends, I will say goodbye to you instead. Stay in peace. The Lord be with you."

I stepped out of the van.

Oh Moksanim! Oh Moksanim! (My name in Korean.) Voices shouted from behind glaring lights. At first I could not comprehend what was going on, but as I was led up the steps to the plane, I looked down into the faces of several young newspaper reporters.

"Don't lose courage!"

"We shall overcome!"

"Your day to return will come swiftly," they shouted at me.

I raised my hand in a benediction. "The Lord God be with you! The Lord give you strength! Long live the people of Korea!"

Then I was on the top step heading into the plane. The immigration man who was leading me directed me toward the

tail of the plane farthest away from the exit. He showed me my
seat and asked if I would sign that the immigration office had
returned my passport to me. (It had been confiscated early that
morning.) I put my hand out to receive the passport.

"I cannot give it to you. I will give it to Captain Kim Ho
Youn (captain of the airplane) and he will give it to you when
you arrive in America."

"I will sign for my passport only when I receive it. Not
before," I replied.

So the captain of the plane signed and took my passport.
How I wished that this could have been avoided. I felt as though
life had been suspended in mid-air. It was all over, and I was
terribly alone. What I had no way of knowing, however, was
that at that very time inside the main terminal a protest demonstration was going on. A hundred and fifty or so friends had
followed us out to the airport. They prayed and sang and
shouted protests against Park Chung Hee, his dictatorship, and
his KCIA.

Once the plane left the ground, my insides collapsed, and
I cried like a baby. Succor came in the form of a Catholic priest,
Vince Alloco. I had known Vince for a couple of years. For
reasons unrelated to me, he was on the same plane. He sat
beside me and literally held my hand across the water to Japan.

By the time we landed in Japan, I had gained control of
myself, so when the loudspeaker announced that all passengers
should deplane, I decided to go to the transient lounge and
stretch my legs. Vince and I stood up, but by the time I got
upright a cabin attendant had placed his hand on my shoulder
and informed me that I was not permitted to leave the plane.
I replied that this was Tokyo, an international airport, and
therefore the KCIA had no jurisdiction over me. I walked down
the aisle. Another cabin attendent came up and repeated the
order. I replied in the same manner that I had before and
entered the little kitchenette, that connects the two aisles of a
747, heading for the exit.

All of a sudden a very large Korean man stood at the exit
side of the kitchenette between me and the door of the airplane.

"Return to your seat! You cannot get off!" he ordered in quiet tones.

"This is international territory. The KCIA has no jurisdiction!" I shouted back.

The two attendants grabbed at me from the rear. I grabbed at the throat of the man in front of me. We pushed and shoved and shouted. I was aware that Oriental and American-like faces were passing us by but no one stopped. They turned their faces away. But then there was a face that I recognized: Captain Kim Ho Youn. I stopped struggling. (Why? I don't know. Perhaps it is my own respect for authority. In that situation he was the chief representative of Park Chung Hee. He is the one I should have wrestled with.) In a quiet voice Kim informed me that I must return to my seat. I would not be allowed to get off the plane. I went back to where my seat was and walked up and down the aisle until it was time to take off again.

My anger would have been even more frustrating if I had known what was going on elsewhere. Two friends were waiting for me just outside the aircraft. I was not ten feet from the exit where I could have seen them, but the KCIA agent had my way blocked.

One of the men was Jim Stentzel, a Methodist missionary journalist. The other was Don Oberdorfer, Tokyo Bureau Chief for the *Washington Post* newspaper. When Father Vince Alloco got off the plane he told Stentzel and Oberdorfer what was happening inside the plane. Alloco went on inside the transient lounge to call the American Embassy in Tokyo. Jim and Don went to the front of the plane and asked to see the captain.

By that time Captain Kim had apparently finished with me at the back of the plane. At first he told Jim and Don that no one by the name of Ogle was on the plane. My name had been omitted from the passenger list. Only after they insisted that they knew I was there did he finally break down and admit I was on board, but he said Mr. Ogle could not leave the aircraft, talk to anyone or contact his embassy. "I am," he said, "under orders from higher authorities to take Mr. Ogle incommunicado to the final destination [Los Angeles]."

"Whose authority?" asked Oberdorfer.

"The highest authority of the Republic of Korea," answered Kim.

"But this is Japan, not Korea," retorted Oberdorfer.

"This (referring to the airplane) is the Republic of Korea!" shouted the captain.

Captain Kim then ordered the two men off his plane. When they refused to go, Japanese police were called. Jim Stentzel speaks Japanese and explained to them that there was an American aboard who was being held prisoner and who wanted to contact the American Embassy in Japan. The Japanese police, however, were not much interested in Americans being held prisoner on a Korean airline. They came about ten feet into the airplane and pushed the two Americans out the door, hustling them off to the police station.

I knew nothing of all of this until Vince Alloco returned. By then it was too late. The doors had closed and we were on our way to Hawaii. Just before we set down in Honolulu, a young Korean man passed my seat and put an envelope into my hands. He hurried on past. I opened the envelope and read: "I must go unnamed, but I am one who looks for the speedy return of free democracy in our land. I know the time will come when you will be asked to return. Please go in health and peace."

Amen and Amen!

EPILOGUE

Official Japanese reaction to my detainment on the Korean airlines at the Tokyo International Airport has been baffling. On December 20th, six days after the incident, Reverend John Nakajima, General Secretary of the National Christian Council of Japan, visited the Tokyo Airport Police Station to inquire about the incident. He was told that their investigation led them to conclude that no one by the name of Ogle was on the airplane. Eleven police, he was told, had searched the entire aircraft calling, "Mr. Ogle, come here," but no one had responded. Nor did the searching police see anyone handcuffed. Therefore, they concluded that I was not on the aircraft.

On February 10, 1975, Ms. Takako Doi, Socialist Party Member of the Japanese Diet, asked a government spokesman at a meeting of the Foreign Relations Committee to explain the Haneda Airport incident of Missionary George Ogle. The answer given by a Mr. Takaoka was to the effect that five policemen tried to find Mr. Ogle in the plane. Some of them called his name in English and some called his name in Japanese, but there was no reply.

A third explanation was given by Mr. Jon Yoshino, Chief of the First Foreign Affairs Section of the Tokyo Metropolitan Police Department on February 13, 1975. At that time I was in Japan, and visited Mr. Yoshino along with Rev. Nakajima. Yoshino's account of the Japanese police behavior agreed basically with that given in the Foreign Relations Committee of the

Japanese Diet, but with one important difference. "The police-men," he said, "may not have gone to the far end of the plane where Mr. Ogle was located."

One of Yoshino's assistants had a different idea. "How much whiskey did you drink between Seoul and Tokyo?" he asked me, insinuating that I was so stone drunk that I could not recognize my own name. I assured him that I do not drink whiskey.

The various Japanese accounts agree on two things: Japanese police searched the plane, calling my name, and secondly, they concluded that I was not on the plane. This, despite the fact that Jim Stentzel swears that no Japanese policemen went beyond ten feet into the plane, and despite the fact that I was indeed on the plane, quite sober, and neither saw nor heard any Japanese policemen at any time. I certainly would have no reason to lie about the police being there. At that particular time, there was no one I would rather have seen than a Japanese policeman calling my name. But there were no Japanese police.

Why would the Japanese police and Japanese foreign ministry concoct such a story? After all I am only a missionary from Korea. I am of no significance to the Japanese government whatsoever. Why such a blatant falsification of the facts? Obviously the Japanese government is fending for the Korean government, but why? After all, it was only about a year previously that the KCIA had shown its disdain for Japan by Kidnapping the popular leader of the Korean democratic forces, Kim Dae Jung, out of a Tokyo hotel. In complete violation of Japanese sovereignty, Kim had been secreted out of Japan and taken back to Korea. Now Japan was protecting the KCIA as it again violated Japanese sovereignty. Why?

The Japanese attitude became more mystifying two months later. The National Christian Council of Japan invited me to return to Japan for a week of speaking. I arrived at the Tokyo airport on February 9, 1975. As I entered the terminal, I was directed to the Office of Immigrations Special Investigation Room. After my identity was verified, I was handed a sheet of paper with English writing on it. The paper, however, had no heading, nor did it have any signature to indicate where it had come from. It read somewhat as follows:

> Your presence in Japan is likely to be used by certain people in an attempt to cause trouble for Japan and the Republic of Korea.
> You are in Japan on a tourist visa. This does not permit you to hold political meetings or speak at political rallies.
> It is hoped that while you are here that you will do nothing to embarass either the government of Japan or the government of the Republic of Korea.

I asked if this were an official order of the Japanese government forbidding me to speak about Korea. I received no answer. I asked if I could take the paper along with me to use it as a guide for my conduct while in Japan. The immigration official grabbed the paper out of my reach.

But why? Why all the defense of the Korean CIA as regards my detention on the plane that night in Tokyo? Why now was the Japanese government going to the unusual lengths of warning me not to talk about the Korean situation? The explanation given by the editor for one of Japan's largest journals was something like this:

You have got to remember that the Japanese government still considers Korea to be a part of its own territory. Park Chung Hee is merely an extension of the Japanese government. He is more Japanese than most Japanese. Japan feels secure with Park in power. Problems develop now and then, of course, but basically the Japanese government feels that Park is their man. In order to prevent any more bad press about the KCIA and the Korean government's violation of Japanese sovereignty, the Japanese police and foreign ministry covered up the incident of your detention at Tokyo by fabricating those absurd stories about the police looking for you. When it was learned that you were to visit Japan, the Korean government asked the Japanese government to keep you out. Since, however, you already had a Japanese visa and you are an American citizen, Japan could not forbid you to come. Instead it indirectly tries to intimidate you into silence.

To me this explanation makes sense. Japan's interest in Korea is another form of its old colonial control over that nation. Park Chung Hee provides a faithful ally, as, of course, do the Americans. Freedom, democratic development, and even re-unification in Korea are all to be measured according to Japanese self-interest. The self-interest and independence of Korea are of minor concern to such powerful people as the Japanese and Americans.

Inside Korea, Park's policy of suppression has accelerated. It is now a crime for Korean citizens to speak unfavorably about their government. Being critical in front of a foreigner could get a Korean seven years in jail. On May 13, 1975, Park issued a ninth emergency decree. All opposition of any form to the *Yushin* system is outlawed. Not only are individual violators liable to punishment, but so are "schools, organizations, and companies to which the violators are attached." No warrant is required to arrest, search or seize, and the decree is made immune from any judicial review. To insure the efficient application of the decree the minister of defense is instructed to assist city and provincial authorities when requested.

The Thursday morning prayer meetings, which have given strength to so many, have been broken up. KCIA agents have forcefully prevented the Christians from meeting even in their own buildings. Catholic priests have been detained and threatened. Masses for social justice and political prisoners have been interfered with and almost stopped.

Not satisfied with these violations against human rights and religious freedom, the Park government on April 13 confiscated financial records of the National Council of Churches and then charged five Korean clergymen with embezzling church funds. Despite the sworn assurance by the National Council of Churches that there had been no mishandling of funds, the KCIA has kept the ministers incarcerated. By doing so, they quiet five leading voices of the church and also sow seeds of distrust or suspicion within the church.

But most tragic of all is the continued persecution of Kim Chi Ha, Korea's heroic young poet, Kim has an obsession with speaking forth the truth in poetic form. Though he is only 32, he has already spent years in prison for his inability to constrain his pen. His sufferings still continue. While in prison in 1974, he found himself in a cell next to Ha Chae Won, an alleged member of the People's Revolutionary Party. In their brief communications with one another, Kim asked, "Tell me, was there really a PRP group?"

"No, the government dreamed it all up."

"Then on what basis are they holding you in prison?"

"The interrogation. They kept at me until I 'confessed.' "

"Was the torture bad?"

"Terrible, brutal. They ruptured my intestines . . . I couldn't stand it. They admitted they were trumping up the whole case. The KCIA said to me, 'We know this is rough on you, but it's a political problem so just try to stand it for a while.' "

Kim was released from prison on February 15, 1975. Immediately he began to write poems about his latest stay in prison. His first poem was about Ha Chae Won:

> Out of the darkness
> someone calls me
> the cell on the far side of the bare
> rust-covered darkness the color of blood
> crouched in the dark, wide open
> two persistent eyes.
>
> Ah—silence calls
> gasps of breath, caught with phlegm,
> call me.
>
> Low grey sky
> drenching the day with constant
> drizzle, ceaselessly
> a voice calls.

Call of the pigeon on the roof
key's sound, trumpet sound, sound
of shoes interrupt it and still,
unceasing,
it calls me.

Tattered underwear stained
with blood hung from
prison bars.

White ghosts writhing
nightly in that room
underground
the screams of many shredded bodies.

Head up, that's it
head up
it calls me . . .
My blood is called to
from the world of silence.

Deny
deny the lie
From out of the pitch-black darkness
low grey sky
drenching the day with constant drizzle
in the darkness of that red, red flesh
wide open those two persistent eyes.

Kim was rearrested. This time the KCIA is apparently determined to bring an end to Kim Chi Ha. He was tortured for five or six days until practically senseless. Unable to take more he wrote down a "confession" dictated to him by a KCIA agent. The "confession" said that Kim Chi Ha was Communist. The penalty for that is death. In a message smuggled out of prison Kim told of the tortures under which this "confession" had been extracted.

He is not a Communist, never has been. But he is a prophet, a man of truth and freedom. From his prison cell he writes:

Nothing is more convenient to those who would spread Communism than the continued existence of this corrupted, privileged and unreasonable dictatorship.

What is necessary for national security is not the perpetuation of dictatorship and oppression. Let us perceive clearly that the only means to true security is to drive out dictatorship and oppression and to defend freedom and democracy. Deprived of freedom and democracy, forced to risk our very lives just to maintain a yoke of despair and humiliation, let us unite our voices in protest!

We are not alone. I trust that freedom—and peace-loving people throughout the world and conscientious neighbors of ours will lend us their tireless support in this most difficult struggle. What our time demands above all is faithfulness and the passion to endure the persecution that will be required of us because of our love for the truth.

For the liberation and freedom of humanity, and for the victory of democracy for which the people hunger and thirst, we want to offer all of ourselves.

I pray this day for a courageous struggle for all of us.

To Park and his KCIA such defiance is intolerable. Those words and the man who speaks them must be eliminated. Therefore, he must be smeared with the stigma of "Communist" and locked in prison or killed. Over two years ago the Prime Minister Kim Chong Pil said he did not think Kim Chi Ha was a Communist.[1] Now, however, the KCIA's failure to break him and Kim's persistent prophesying have changed the government's mind. One free man like Kim Chi Ha is a threat to Park Chung Hee, Kim Chong Pil, and the KCIA. Freedom in a person is dangerous to a state that seeks total submissiveness from its people.

But freedom and prophesying, especially when combined with a Christian faith, are not as easily eliminated as Park might think, even if a man is killed. Kim speaks for many other Christians when he writes:

At present I am denied the right to receive visitors or communications, to write, or even read the Bible. This tightly closed cell of total darkness has a space of about 48 square feet. In this darkness, with my eyes glaring in anger, I am constantly challenging an ill-omened grey future. The agony of this provides me with a limitless fuel to keep my fighting spirit burning, so that I do not fall asleep in front of the enemy.

NOTES

Chapter 4
1. *Business Week,* September 1, 1973, p. 50.
2. *Ibid.,* p. 52.
3. Don Barlett and James Steele, "Foreign Aid: The Flawed Dream," Part 4, *Philadelphia Inquirer,* November 24–29, 1974.

Chapter 5
1. Richard Halloran, "Seoul's Vast Intelligence Agency Stirs Wide Fear," *New York Times,* August 20, 1973, p. 3.
2. *Ibid.*
3. *Time* Magazine, November 29, 1976, p. 14; "Korea's Bribery" (editorial); *Washington Post,* October 27, 1976.

Epilogue
1. *Newsweek,* August 12, 1974. Interview with Paul Brinkley-Rogers.